500

ice creams,
sorbets & gelatos

500

ice creams,
sorbets & gelatos

the only ice cream compendium you'll ever need

Alex Barker

SELLERS
PUBLISHING

A Quintet Book

Published by Sellers Publishing, Inc.
P.O. Box 818, Portland, Maine 04104
For ordering information:
(800) 625-3386 Toll Free
(207) 772-6814 Fax
Visit our Web site: www.rsvp.com • E-mail: rsp@rsvp.com

ISBN: 978-1-4162-0533-3
Library of Congress Control Number: 2008933664
QTT.ISO

This book was designed and produced by
Quintet Publishing Limited
6 Blundell Street
London N7 9BH
United Kingdom

Project Editor: Robert Davies
Designer: Dean Martin
Copy Editor: Cary Hull
Photography: Alex Barker, Dave Jordan
Food Styling: Sophie Northcote-Smith, Louise Halswell
Art Director: Michael Charles
Managing Editor: Donna Gregory
Publisher: James Tavendale

10 9 8 7 6 5 4 3 2 1

Printed in China by SNP Leefung Printers Ltd.

The author would like to thank the following manufacturers for
the loan of ice cream machines to help with creating and testing
recipes: Phillips, Kenwood, Cuisinart, and Magimix.

contents

introduction

Over the years, books have related numerous tales of the origins of ice cream — how the Roman Emperor Nero would send slaves to the mountains to collect snow to mix with fruit and honey; how Marco Polo discovered it on his travels in China in the thirteenth century; and how Charles I served a newly created sweet frozen dessert at a royal banquet in seventeenth-century England. We've been told that George Washington and Thomas Jefferson served ice cream at presidential banquets, that the first ice cream parlor opened in New York in 1770, and that the waffle cone was created in the early twentieth century.

Ice cream has come a long way over the centuries. It's been Americanized with all sorts of added goodies (cookie dough, candies, peanut butter, and countless more). It's been made rich and velvety smooth and sophisticated by the French with their creamy egg custards. In Italy, it's gelato — a simpler version using mainly milk, plus eggs and cream. Middle Eastern sherbet or *serbet* (a drink of water sweetened with fruit or fruit purée and frozen) has become sorbet, which in America is generally enriched with milk. Ask for a sorbet in Italy, and you may get the softer-textured water ice, which can also go by the name "granita." Granita — the very granular or slushy frozen fruit ice — is said to come from Sicily, where it is served almost as a drink.

But who cares about a name when you're licking the dribbles off a creamy ice cream cone, biting into a hot-cold baked Alaska, or diving into a sprinkle-and-whipped-cream-topped banana split? Chocoholics just want to be treated to the richest chocolate ice cream around. Hot Sunday afternoons call out for a delicate jasmine tea sorbet. The kick of lemon granita is just what's needed to cleanse the palate during a five-course dinner. And kids will love to try their hand at decorating ice cream cupcakes or blitzing frozen smoothies. Maybe ice creams bring back happy childhood memories, or perhaps you're just a sucker for their sweet cool creaminess or tongue-tingling fruity tang. Whatever the case, you're bound to find ideas in this book to tempt you again and again.

making ice cream

Making ice cream, at its simplest, is a matter of beating cream, eggs, sugar, and flavorings together and stirring this mixture frequently while it freezes. This is easily done by hand, though you'll need to set aside about 4 or 5 hours to do so. An electric ice cream maker will save time and effort, and it does produce a softer, smoother, and creamier result.

ice cream makers

There are many ice cream machines available today to fit all price brackets. The simplest consist of a bucket container that needs to be frozen for at least 24 hours in advance, creating an aluminum ice bucket. This is fitted into a base with an electric paddle top and enclosed lid. When you turn on the machine and pour in the mixture, it churns inside the pre-iced bucket until sufficiently frozen. The fully automatic machines are large, heavy, and costly, because they have a built-in cooling system. You don't have to prefreeze the bucket and you can buy one with a timer, so you can switch it on and leave it. You still need to be ready at the end, however, to decant the frozen ice quickly into a container for the final minutes of freezing or for storage.

basic hand-mixing method

It is the blending and whisking that gives the smooth creamy finish we associate with a really good ice cream. If you use an ice cream maker, your ice cream will have 30 to 40 minutes of consistent stirring or churning. Making it by hand can produce as good a result but with some more effort.

The ingredients for hand-mixed ice cream should be well chilled before they're combined. The mixture is then poured into a freezer container deep enough to allow space for later mixing. The container needs to be covered with a sheet of plastic wrap or waxed paper so it can freeze more evenly, and then topped with a well-fitting lid. Place the container in the coldest part of a really cold freezer. Leave for about 1 hour; then, using a fork, scrape the frozen ice cream in from the edges, and then whisk to a smooth, even texture. Cover the container again and return to the freezer for another hour. Repeat this process once or twice more at least, until the ice cream is smooth and nearly evenly frozen. Then cover and leave it to freeze completely.

marbling & rippling

Marbled or rippled ice creams look terrific and give the bonus of extra flavor. To make one, prepare the ice cream in a machine or by hand. Then, as you transfer it to a freezer container (or after the final stirring of a hand-mixed ice cream), spoon on the rippling or marbling ingredient or sauce and fold it in just a couple of times. Do not stir it through. The real marbling and rippling effect is acquired when you later scoop out the ice cream.

molding & shaping

When ice cream is sufficiently mixed and firm but not frozen hard, it can be put into a shaped container or mold, but work quickly because it will be softening all the time. Be sure to make the top completely flat and scrape away any excess from the edges so it's easier to unmold. Cover with waxed paper and refreeze as soon as possible. It is also helpful to line any molds or pans with plastic wrap for easy removal.

piping

Ice cream can be piped if it is a perfectly smooth recipe, with no seeds or texture, and if it is well frozen but not solid. Place a small quantity in a piping bag with a fluted nozzle and pipe swirls quickly into a chilled dish, cupcake liners, or onto serving wafers and return to the freezer immediately. Only do a small quantity at a time, because your hands on the bag will speed up melting time.

scooping & serving

Most ice creams are best almost as soon as they are made, as long as they've had 15 to 20 minutes in the freezer to firm up before you scoop out servings. Once an ice cream has frozen hard, you will need to allow 10 to 15 minutes at room temperature – or at least 30 minutes in the refrigerator – to soften sufficiently to scoop. It's a good idea to chill your serving dishes in advance. Once an ice cream has been fully defrosted, it should not be returned to the freezer. Ice creams rarely improve with keeping; they often just get harder.

There are two types of scoop – the round spring-loaded scoop, and the oval half spoon. The latter produces small shapes and half scoops. The spring-loaded variety comes in different sizes, from melon ball size to small tennis ball size. To get a good scoop, dip the head in water, shake off the excess, and pull the scoop over the surface of the ice cream, allowing it to roll inside the scoop and make a good shape. If there's time, place the scooped ice cream on a baking sheet or directly into serving dishes and refreeze until it firms up again.

storing

Homemade ice creams are not designed for long storage. A maximum of a day or two is ideal, especially for an ice with a high water and fruit content, because they get harder with time. Obviously, it is lovely to be able to turn a glut of fresh berries into a delicious batch of sorbet for the freezer. In this case add a piece of plastic wrap along the top of the ice cream, under the container lid, and don't open until required. Cream-based mixtures can be stored longer; check the recipes for storage recommendations.

other equipment

An electric blender or food processor is useful for mixing and whisking. Measuring cups and spoons will ensure you get your quantities right, and a supply of freezer containers with tight-fitting lids will be needed to store the ice creams. Plastic scrapers and spoons are vital if you are using an ice cream machine so you don't scratch the aluminum container.

ingredients

Very few ingredients are used in making ice cream, but their quality is crucial to the flavor of the end product, especially because there is little or no cooking involved.

eggs
For the recipes in this book, use large eggs, preferably free-range and date stamped so you know how old they are. While very fresh eggs don't produce a good volume of whisked egg whites, you should avoid using eggs that are more than 8 to 10 days old, especially if they will not be cooked. Pregnant women are advised not to eat ice cream containing raw eggs.

milk & cream
Most recipes in this book use whole milk or heavy cream. Lower-fat products can be substituted if you prefer, but nonfat and very low-fat products are not recommended for ice creams, except in the chapters at the end of the book.

sugar, sugar syrup & flavored syrup
Most recipes use superfine sugar, because it dissolves easily, but granulated sugar can be substituted. Most ice creams can also be made with light or dark brown sugar, or you can use honey and light corn syrup. Experiment to find your preferred sweetness. Artifical sweeteners can be used; follow the package instructions, at least the first time you try them.

Many ices and sorbets require a sugar syrup. Mix 1 cup granulated sugar with 1 cup water to make approximately 1 1/2 cups sugar syrup. In a small saucepan, heat the sugar gently in the water until fully dissolved, then bring to a boil and simmer for a couple of minutes or until slightly syrupy. Cool, then refrigerate no longer than a day until ready to use; if refrigerated for longer it will crystallize. Or, store in a covered jar in a cool dark place.

Occasionally a recipe calls for a flavored syrup. For vanilla syrup, add 1 vanilla pod, cut open to release the seeds. For lemon syrup, add 2 or 3 large strips of lemon zest (no pith, just the yellow rind). For chile syrup, add 1 small red chile, seeds discarded. Add the flavoring when you start dissolving the sugar in the water. Remove the flavoring when the syrup is cold.

Although it is possible to buy coffee syrup, homemade coffee syrup gives a truer and subtler flavor. Dissolve 1/3 cup light brown sugar in 1/2 cup very strong espresso, then simmer gently until reduced to about 3 to 4 tablespoons or the strength you prefer. Don't boil hard, because this can produce a bitter flavor. Chill and store as above.

flavorings & fruits

It is best to buy ice cream flavorings fresh for the recipe. Use vanilla pods or a pure vanilla extract, not a synthetic extract. The best chocolate has a high cocoa solid content, so read the package before you buy — look for at least 60 percent, preferably unsweetened. Nuts are used in many recipes; be sure they are fresh and firm. When fruit or berries are used in the ice cream, use the most unblemished, perfectly ripe fruit you can find. Ripe fruit and berries at their peak give the sweetest, best flavor, which is just what you need for ice cream. Frozen fruit and berries can be used for some sorbets and can give very quick and delicious results.

fruit purées

Sorbets, water ices, and granitas depend on a good fruit purée. Any well-flavored fruit can be used to make a purée. Avoid cooking the fruit if possible, because cooking destroys the fresh fruit flavor. Purée the prepared fruit (peel if the skin is tough, and remove pits, seeds, and stalks as necessary) in a blender or food processor. If the fruit is one that discolors easily, add lemon juice. Strain or push through a sieve only if you want a really smooth result, because this removes much of the body and texture from an ice cream.

sauces & toppings

Your homemade ice creams, sorbets, and gelatos will be delicious on their own, but they also can be topped with a fruit, chocolate, or butterscotch sauce; decorated with sprinkles, grated chocolate, marshmallows, chopped fruit, or crushed cookies; or dressed up with homemade praline or caramel.

chocolate sauce
Break 8 ounces dark, milk, or white chocolate into small pieces. Put the broken chocolate in a heatproof bowl. Heat 1/2 cup heavy cream in a small pan until it is almost boiling. Pour the cream over the chocolate, stirring until the chocolate is melted, and then stir in 4 tablespoons unsalted butter. Mix until smooth and runny. Serve hot or cooled, or store in a screwtop jar in the refrigerator for up to 8 days. Makes 1 3/4 cups.

toffee or butterscotch sauce
Heat 1/2 cup unsalted butter, 1/2 cup light brown sugar, and 1/2 cup light corn syrup together in a saucepan until the sugar has dissolved and the mixture is well blended. Bring to a boil and let bubble gently for 3 or 4 minutes. Remove from the heat and stir in 1/2 cup heavy cream and 1/2 teaspoon pure vanilla extract. Mix well and serve, or store in a screwtop jar in the refrigerator for up to 8 days. Makes 1 3/4 cups.

chocolate fudge sauce
To make a delicious chocolatey fudge sauce, follow the recipe for toffee sauce but cook the butter, sugar, and corn syrup for several minutes longer until it becomes quite fudgy. Remove from the heat, and stir in the cream, vanilla, and 1/2 cup broken-up semisweet chocolate. Keep stirring until well blended and smooth. Makes 1 3/4 cups.

fruit sauces

For a fresh berry sauce, mash 1/2 cup fresh, ripe berries with 1/4 cup (adjust to taste) superfine sugar. Then push through a sieve to give a smooth sauce. Use immediately or chill in a screwtop jar in the refrigerator for a few days.

Soft fruits such as mango, apricot, nectarine, peach, and even pineapple can quickly be made into a sauce by blitzing in a blender or food processor with sugar to taste and 4 to 5 tablespoons lemon or orange juice.

caramel

Pure caramel makes a great decoration when crushed into small pieces or carefully broken into dramatically large shards. Sprinkle 1/4 cup granulated sugar evenly onto a sheet of foil on a baking pan. Place the pan into a medium-hot (400°F/200°C) oven, turning it and swirling the sugar around once or twice so it settles evenly. Cook for 6 to 8 minutes, until the sugar is melted and golden. Remove and cool until brittle, then break up into long shards or small pieces. Keep in an airtight container for a short time (a day or two depending on the atmosphere). For a fruit version, sprinkle small fruits such as blueberries or black currants onto the warm sugar so they settle into the sheet of caramel.

praline

Praline is caramel with almost any type of nuts added. Try making praline with almonds, hazelnuts, pecans, pistachios, or mixed nuts. It is used broken into large pieces, lightly crushed to sprinkle over ice creams, or finely ground to mix into recipes. Heat 1 cup superfine sugar and 1 cup shelled, whole, unsalted nuts carefully in a clean, heavy-based pan, while the sugar dissolves. Cook gently, stirring occasionally, until the sugar turns light golden, then remove immediately from the heat and tip the praline straight onto a sheet of foil or parchment and leave until cooled and firm.

cookies & accompaniments

Cookies are not only delicious to eat with ice cream, some also can be shaped into cones, cigars, or cups to hold or dress up ice cream. You have to work quickly, wrapping or draping still-soft, warm cookies around your chosen shaping tools. For cones, wrap the soft cookie around a cone-shaped mold or shape by hand, then hold the cookie until it's firm enough not to unroll. For cigars, roll the soft cookie around a wooden spoon handle or, for a larger version, wrap loosely over a rolling pin. For cups, drape the soft cookie over upturned cups or ramekins, then flute and shape slightly.

chocolate cups

These cups are quick to make and are great for serving ice cream. They can be stored for up to 4 weeks in an airtight container in a cool, dry place. To make them, melt 4 ounces bittersweet chocolate. Using either a double layer of paper cupcake liners or reusable silicone cupcake liners, paint the inside of 6 with a thick, even layer of the chocolate. Turn them upside down on a board or baking pan and let set. When they are hard, carefully peel away the liners and neaten the top edges.

wafers

Wafer cones have been used for serving ice cream since the early nineteenth century, and they remain the most popular way of enjoying a scoop of ice cream on the move. Thin, flat wafers with a waffle pattern stamped on the surface can also be used to make ice cream sandwiches; or look out for fan-shaped wafers which make an excellent edible decoration for sundaes served in tall glasses.

tuiles

Make these pretty curved biscuits to go with the more delicately flavored ices and sorbets.

2 egg whites
1/2 cup superfine sugar
3 tbsp all-purpose flour, sifted
1 tbsp. cornstarch, sifted
3 tbsp. butter, melted
2 tsp. orange or lemon zest or 2 tbsp. sliced almonds (optional)

Preheat the oven to 425°F (220°C). Line baking pans with nonstick baking paper and set out your shaping tools. Whisk the egg whites until stiff, then gradually whisk in the sugar, flour, and cornstarch. Pour in the butter in a fine stream and fold in gently along with any flavoring. Place a few spoonfuls of batter well apart on the baking pan. Flatten out with the back of a spoon as thinly as possible. Bake for 5 to 7 minutes or until the edges begin to turn brown. Remove from the oven and lift straight off the pans with a flat spatula. Shape immediately because they harden quickly. Makes about 30.

freezer cookies

Keep a batch of this cookie dough in the freezer, rolled into a cylinder shape and wrapped in foil. Then you can slice cookies onto a baking pan, or add the uncooked dough straight into an ice cream.

4 tbsp. (1/2 stick) unsalted butter or margarine, softened
1/3 cup confectioners' sugar
1 egg, beaten
1 tsp. pure vanilla extract
1 cup all-purpose flour, sifted
1 tsp. baking powder

Cream the butter and sugar together until light and fluffy. Gradually work in the egg and vanilla. Knead in the flour and baking powder to make a soft dough. Add flavoring if you wish — 2 to 3 teaspoons finely grated lemon or orange rind, or 1 tablespoon unsweetened cocoa powder (replacing 1 tablespoon flour). Chill until firm. Form a long roll and freeze until required, or roll out on a floured surface and cut into circles or shapes, as you wish. Place on baking sheets and bake in a preheated 350°F (175°C) oven for 12 to 15 minutes until firm. They will crisp up as they cool. Makes about 20.

ginger snaps (also called brandy snaps)

These crunchy, spicy, and lacy cookies can also be shaped in various ways to serve ice creams and sorbets in or with. I often serve ice cream in ginger baskets (see photo on page 117).

1/2 cup (1 stick) unsalted butter
1 cup superfine sugar
4 tbsp. light corn syrup
1/2 cup all-purpose flour
1 tsp. ground ginger (or 1 tsp. finely grated lemon zest or 2 tsp. brandy)

Preheat the oven to 350°F (175°C). Melt the butter, sugar, and corn syrup in a medium saucepan until the ingredients are dissolved and well blended. Remove from the heat and cool slightly, then beat in the flour and flavoring of your choice. Drop teaspoonfuls about 3 to 4 inches apart on baking pans and bake only 3 or 4 at a time for 6 to 7 minutes until golden and bubbly. Remove from the oven, lift off the pans with a flat spatula, and shape immediately because they harden quickly. Makes about 20.

classic ice creams

How will you be able to choose between all these lip-smacking ice cream favorites? There's chunky rocky road, crunchy butter pecan, crumbly fudge brownie, sticky peanut butter, dark chocolate chip, tangy New York cheesecake, and more. Or just make them all!

vanilla ice cream

see variations page 38

This is a delicious yet deceptively simple ice cream made, as it sounds, almost entirely from icy cold cream and milk. If you wish to make it richer, add a raw egg yolk with the whipped cream.

1/3 cup superfine sugar
2 cups whole milk, chilled
2 tsp. pure vanilla extract
1 cup heavy cream, whipped and chilled

Over low heat, warm the sugar in a saucepan with half the milk until the sugar has dissolved. Stir in the vanilla and let cool.

Mix in the whipped cream. Pour into an ice cream maker and process according to the manufacturer's directions. Churn for about 40 minutes or until almost firm, then transfer to a freezer container. Freeze for 15 minutes before serving. If you do not have an ice cream maker, follow the hand-mixing method on page 8.

Store in the freezer for up to 3 months; take out 15 minutes before serving to soften.

Makes about 1 1/4 pints

rich chocolate ice cream

see variations page 39

A good chocolate ice cream, quickly made, is the perfect treat to end any meal.

1/3 cup superfine sugar
2 cups whole milk, chilled
1/4 cup unsweetened cocoa powder

1/2 cup dark chocolate, broken up
2 tsp. pure vanilla extract
1 cup heavy cream, whipped and chilled

Warm the sugar in a pan with half the milk, the cocoa powder, and the dark chocolate, stirring occasionally. When the chocolate is completely dissolved and well blended, set aside to cool completely.

When cold, stir in the vanilla and the rest of the milk. Whisk this mixture gradually into the whipped cream. Pour into an ice cream maker and process according to the manufacturer's directions. Churn for about 20 minutes or until almost firm, and then transfer to a freezer container. Freeze for 15 minutes before serving. If you do not have an ice cream maker, follow the hand-mixing method on page 8.

This ice cream can be stored in the freezer for up to 1 month. Take out 15 minutes before serving to soften.

Makes about 1 1/4 pints

new york cheesecake ice cream

see variations page 40

Thick, creamy, lemon cheesecake makes a fabulous ice cream mixture, especially with a swirl of buttery graham cracker crumbs to echo the texture of a cheesecake base.

1 8-oz package cream cheese
finely grated zest and juice of 1 large unwaxed
    lemon
1/3 cup superfine sugar

2 egg yolks
1 cup heavy or whipping cream, whipped
4 tbsp. (1/2 stick) butter, melted
1/2 cup graham cracker crumbs

Beat together all the ingredients, except the butter and graham cracker crumbs, until smooth. Taste, and add more sugar if you prefer it sweeter.

Pour into an ice cream maker and follow the manufacturer's freezing directions. Churn the ice cream for about 30 minutes or until nearly firm. If you do not have an ice cream maker, follow the hand-mixing method on page 8.

Meanwhile, mix the melted butter and crumbs together thoroughly. Cool.

When the ice cream is nearly firm, tip into a freezer container, add the crumbs, and stir just once or twice, to swirl or ripple rather than mix evenly. Freeze until firm or ready to serve.

Store in the freezer for up to 3 months; take out 15 minutes before serving to soften.

Makes about 1 1/4 pints

cookies & cream ice cream

see variations page 41

Imagine your favorite cookies with lashings of cream, made into an ice cream.

1 cup whole milk
1/3 cup superfine sugar
1 tsp. pure vanilla extract

1 1/2 cups heavy cream
1 cup crumbled Oreo cookies

Over low heat, warm the milk, sugar, and vanilla together in a saucepan, stirring until the sugar has dissolved. Let cool, then chill in the refrigerator.

Whip the cream until thick and then whisk in the chilled milk mixture. Pour into an ice cream maker and process according to the manufacturer's directions. If you do not have an ice cream maker, follow the instructions on page 8.

Freeze until the ice cream is nearly firm, then add the crumbled cookies and stir through gently. Place the ice cream in the freezer for about 15 minutes before serving. Store in the freezer for up to 3 months, take out 15 minutes before serving to soften.

Makes about 1 1/2 pints

fudge brownie ice cream

see variations page 12

This one's very rich, so don't make it when anyone is thinking of dieting!

1/4 cup superfine sugar
1 1/2 cups whole milk, chilled
2 tsp. pure vanilla extract

1 cup heavy cream, whipped and chilled
1/3 recipe fudge sauce (page 13)
2 large chocolate brownies, broken into chunks

Blend the sugar into 1/2 cup milk, pour into a small saucepan, and warm through until the sugar has dissolved. Stir in the vanilla and let cool.

Gently beat together the cooled milk, whipped cream, and chocolate fudge sauce. Pour into an ice cream maker and process according to the manufacturer's directions, or pour into a freezer container and freeze using the hand-mixing method on page 8.

When the ice cream is almost firm, stir in chunks of brownies and freeze until ready to serve. Store in the freezer for up to 3 months, but take out 15 minutes before serving to soften. Serve with a little more fudge sauce if you wish.

Makes about 1 1/4 pints

crunchy peanut butter ice cream

see variations page 43

Peanut butter lovers will go crazy for this peanut-packed ice cream—make it as smooth or as crunchy as you like!

1 cup whole milk
2/3 cup granulated sugar
1 tsp. pure vanilla extract

1 cup crunchy peanut butter
2 cups whipping or heavy cream, whipped
2 tbsp. chopped unsalted peanuts

Over low heat, warm the milk in a small pan with the sugar and vanilla. Set aside to cool completely.

Gently beat the cooled milk into the peanut butter to blend well, then fold in the whipped cream.

Pour the mixture into an ice cream maker and process according to the manufacturer's instructions, or pour into a freezer container and follow the hand-mixing method (page 8). When the ice cream is almost firm, add the extra nuts. Freeze for 15 minutes before serving.

This ice cream can be stored in the freezer for up to 3 months. Take it out 15 minutes before serving to soften.

Makes about 1 3/4 pints

rum & raisin ice cream

see variations page 44

Sweet and fruity, with a little kick of rum for special occasions.

1/4 cup lightly chopped raisins
1/4 cup rum
1/4 cup superfine sugar
2 cups whole milk, chilled

1 tsp. pure vanilla extract
2 egg yolks
1 cup heavy cream, whipped and chilled

Soak the raisins in the rum for a couple of hours.

Blend the sugar into half the milk and warm through over low heat until the sugar has dissolved. Whisk in the rest of the milk, the vanilla, and the egg yolks. Let cool completely.

Whisk the cooled milk mixture into the whipped cream. Pour into an ice cream maker and process according to the manufacturer's directions, or into a freezer container and follow the hand-mixing method (page 8).

Halfway through, add the soaked raisins and continue churning until firm or stir them into the mixture in the freezer container and return to the freezer until firm. Freeze for 15 minutes before serving or until required.

This ice cream can be frozen for up to 3 months. Take it out 15 minutes before serving to soften.

Makes about 1 3/4 pints

rocky road ice cream

see variations page 45

If you can't find mini-marshmallows, use the larger ones and snip them into smaller pieces with wet scissors.

1/3 cup superfine sugar
2 cups whole milk, chilled
1/4 cup unsweetened cocoa powder
1/2 milk chocolate, broken up
2 tsp. pure vanilla extract

1 cup heavy cream, whipped and chilled
1 cup mini-marshmallows
1/2 cup mixed roughly chopped pecans and
  sliced almonds

Warm the sugar in a pan with half the milk, the cocoa powder, and the chocolate, stirring occasionally. When the chocolate is completely dissolved and the mixture is well blended, set aside to cool completely.

When cooled, stir in the vanilla and the rest of the milk. Whisk this gradually into the whipped cream.

Pour into an ice cream maker and process according to the manufacturer's directions. When almost frozen, tip the ice cream into a freezer container, and quickly stir in the marshmallows and nuts. If you do not have an ice cream maker, follow the hand-mixing method on page 8 and stir in the marshmallows and nuts after whisking the ice cream for the last time. Freeze for 15 minutes before serving or until required.

Store in the freezer for up to 2 weeks but take out 15 minutes before serving to soften.

Makes about 1 3/4 pints

butter pecan ice cream

see variations page 46

This ice cream is totally irresistible with a buttery toffee flavor and a nutty crunchy texture. If you like the slightly stronger, more bitter flavor of walnuts, you could always try using those instead.

2 egg yolks
1/3 cup light brown sugar
1 1/2 cups light cream
1/2 cup heavy cream

few drops pure vanilla extract
4 tbsp. butter
1/2 cup roughly chopped pecans
2/3 cup light brown sugar

Beat the egg yolks, brown sugar, and light cream together until thick, then beat in the heavy cream and vanilla. Pour the mixture into an ice cream maker and freeze according to the manufacturer's instructions, or follow the hand-mixing method (page 8).

Meanwhile, place the butter in a saucepan with the nuts and brown sugar and cook over low heat, stirring frequently, until the sugar has completely dissolved and looks like toffee. Be very careful it does not burn. Remove from the heat immediately, take out half, and set it aside to cool completely. Leave the rest in the pan to reheat later for the topping.

When the ice cream is nearly firm, crumble in the cooled butter pecan mixture and continue mixing for only a few minutes. Freeze for at least 15 minutes before serving. Serve topped with warmed butter pecan topping. This ice cream can be frozen for up to 3 months; take out 15 minutes before serving to soften.

Makes about 1 pint

blueberry muffin ice cream

see variations page 47

The tangy flavor of blueberries is the perfect complement for the creamy richness of ice cream.

1/4 cup superfine sugar
2 cups whole milk
2 tsp. pure vanilla extract
1 cup heavy cream, whipped and chilled

2 egg yolks
2 blueberry muffins, crumbled
1/4 cup fresh blueberries

In a saucepan, blend the sugar into half the milk, then warm through until the sugar has dissolved. Stir in the vanilla and let cool.

Beat the cooled milk with the whipped cream, egg yolks, and crumbled muffins. Pour into an ice cream maker and process following the manufacturer's directions. Churn for about 30 minutes or until almost firm, stir in the fresh blueberries, and transfer to a freezer container. Freeze for 15 minutes before serving or until required.

If you do not have an ice cream maker, use the hand-mixing method (page 8). Stir in the fresh blueberries after whisking the ice cream for the last time. Return to the freezer until required.

Store the ice cream in the freezer for up to 3 months. Take it out 15 minutes before serving to soften.

Makes about 1 3/4 pints

variations

vanilla ice cream

see base recipe page 19

strawberry ice cream
Purée 3 cups chopped strawberries with 1/2 cup superfine sugar. Strain to remove seeds. Prepare the basic vanilla ice cream, and, when almost firm, blend in the purée.

praline ice cream
Prepare the basic vanilla ice cream. When it is almost firm, mix in 6 tablespoons roughly crushed praline (page 14).

honeycomb ice cream
When the basic vanilla ice cream is almost firm, add 1/2 cup roughly crushed honeycomb candy.

neapolitan ice cream
Prepare one recipe each of the basic vanilla, strawberry variation, and rich chocolate ice creams (pages 19, above, and 20). As each ice cream is finished, spread it in a plastic wrap-lined 8 1/2 x 4 1/2-inch loaf pan and let freeze. Then make the next ice cream and spread it on top of the first one. Chill until just frozen and serve in slices.

variations

rich chocolate ice cream

see base recipe page 20

double chocolate chip ice cream
Prepare the basic ice cream recipe and just before freezing stir in
3 tablespoons each of white and dark chocolate chips.

chocolate chile ice cream
When making the basic ice cream add 1/2 teaspoon (or 1 teaspoon if you
like some real kick!) dried chile flakes to the milk, cocoa, and sugar mixture.

white chocolate ice cream with dark chocolate chips
Prepare the basic ice cream using 1 1/2 cups of broken up white chocolate
instead of both the cocoa powder and the dark chocolate. Prepare as in
the base recipe, then stir in at the last minute 3 tablespoons of dark
chocolate chips.

rich chocolate & cookie dough ice cream
Prepare the basic recipe, stirring in 1/2 cup uncooked cookie dough
(page 16) before the ice cream is completely frozen.

variations

new york cheesecake ice cream

see base recipe page 23

strawberry cheesecake ice cream
When the basic ice cream is almost frozen, stir in 1/2 cup chopped ripe strawberries. Continue stirring just a few minutes more, then set in the freezer to freeze completely.

blueberry cheesecake ice cream
Prepare the basic ice cream and, when almost frozen, stir in 1/2 cup fresh blueberries. Continue stirring for only a few minutes more, then set in the freezer to freeze completely.

fudge & almond swirl cheesecake ice cream
Prepare the basic ice cream until quite firm, then gently fold in 3 tablespoons toasted sliced almonds and 4 tablespoons fudge sauce (page 13). Don't stir too much.

coffee & ginger cheesecake ice cream
Prepare the basic ice cream until almost frozen, then add 1/4 cup chopped stem ginger and 3 tablespoons coffee syrup (page 12).

variations

cookies & cream ice cream

see base recipe page 24

vanilla cookies & cream ice cream
Prepare the basic ice cream, replacing the cookies with vanilla cookies.

meringues & cream ice cream
Replace the cookies in the basic ice cream, with 1 cup crushed meringues.

breakfast cookies & cream ice cream
Prepare the basic ice cream. When you add the cookies, add 1 tablespoon raisins and 1 tablespoon toasted oats (cooled).

strawberry ripple ice cream
When you add the cookies to the basic ice cream, gently stir in 2 tablespoons lightly mashed strawberries.

cookie dough & cream ice cream
Prepare the basic ice cream, replacing the crumbled cookies with uncooked cookie dough (page 16). Or work together 1 tablespoon butter with 2 tablespoons all-purpose flour and a drop of vanilla extract, and add to the mixture in small lumps.

variations

fudge brownie ice cream

see base recipe page 27

fruity fudge brownie ice cream

Prepare the basic ice cream, but stir in the fudge sauce after the churning stage along with 1/2 cup dried blueberries, cranberries, or cherries, and just 1 piece of crumbled brownie.

white fudge blondie ice cream

Prepare the basic recipe, but stir in the fudge sauce, 3 tablespoons white chocolate chunks, and 2 crumbled blond brownies when the ice cream is almost firm.

almond nugget brownie ice cream

When preparing the basic ice cream omit the fudge sauce and stir in 1/2 cup finely chopped white (natural) almond paste along with the chocolate brownies.

mississippi fudge brownie ice cream

Prepare the basic ice cream, but don't add the sauce or brownies. Divide the mixture into two bowls. Add the fudge sauce to one bowl, then freeze. To the other bowl, add 1/4 cup chopped marshmallows and freeze. When the two parts are almost frozen, layer in one container.

crunchy peanut butter ice cream

see base recipe page 28

crunchy peanut butter & banana chip ice cream
Prepare the basic ice cream, adding 1/8 cup broken-up dried banana chips in the last few minutes of mixing.

peanut butter & jelly ice cream
Before the basic ice cream is fully set, stir or swirl through it 1/4 cup raspberry jam or jelly.

peanut butter & white chocolate ice cream
Prepare the basic ice cream and before it is quite set stir in 1/4 cup white chocolate chunks.

peanut butter extra honey roasted ice cream
Before the basic ice cream is fully set, stir in 1/4 cup roughly chopped honey-roasted peanuts.

peanut butter & chewy mallow ice cream
Prepare the basic recipe, stirring in 1/2 cup halved mini-marshmallows just before the final freezing.

variations

rum & raisin ice cream

see base recipe page 31

rum & raisin ice cream with toasted hazelnuts
When the basic ice cream is nearly frozen, stir in 1/4 cup
chopped toasted hazelnuts.

rum & raisin ice cream with candied fruits
Prepare the basic ice cream and when nearly frozen stir in 1/4 cup
chopped crystallized fruits (ginger, pineapple, or candied peel).

rum & raisin with chocolate-coated cranberries
When the basic ice cream is nearly frozen, stir in 1/4 cup chocolate-coated
cranberries or dried cranberries.

rum & raisin ice cream with clotted cream
Prepare the basic ice cream, replacing the second cup of milk with
clotted cream. Serve with clotted cream on top.

rum & raisin ice cream with extra berries
Prepare the basic recipe, stirring in 1/4 cup dried berries (such as
blueberries, cranberries, or cherries) just before the final freezing.

variations

rocky road ice cream

see base recipe page 32

nut-free rocky road ice cream
Prepare the basic recipe, replacing the nuts with 1/2 cup chopped dried
fruits (such as apricots, candied ginger, or pineapple).

honeycomb rocky road ice cream
Replace all or half the marshmallows in the basic recipe with
broken pieces of honeycomb candy.

rocky road toblerone ice cream
Prepare the basic recipe, replacing the nuts with broken pieces of nutty
dark chocolate Toblerone.

rainbow rocky road ice cream
Prepare the basic recipe but replace half the marshmallows and half the
nuts with 1/2 cup M&Ms or any other multicolored candies.

really nutty rocky road ice cream
Add an extra 1/2 cup toasted sliced almonds or chopped peanuts to the
basic recipe.

variations

butter pecan ice cream

see base recipe page 35

butter pecan & maple syrup ice cream
Prepare the basic ice cream, making only half the butter pecan mixture and using maple syrup in it instead of brown sugar. Serve drizzled with more maple syrup instead of the butter pecan topping.

butter pecan & date ice cream
Prepare the basic ice cream, adding 4 tablespoons chopped pitted dates to the butter pecan mixture.

butter pecan with coffee ripple ice cream
When the basic ice cream is almost set fold or stir in 2 to 3 tablespoons coffee syrup (page 12).

butter pecan & berry ice cream
Prepare the basic ice cream, adding 2 tablespoons dried berries (preferably a mixture of cranberries, cherries, and blueberries) when almost firm.

variations

blueberry muffin ice cream

see base recipe page 36

white chocolate chip muffin ice cream
Replace the fresh blueberries of the basic ice cream with 2 ounces of chopped white chocolate.

extra-fruity muffin ice cream
Prepare the basic ice cream, substituting 1/2 cup dried berries for the fresh blueberries.

roasted cranberry muffin ice cream
Mix 1/2 cup fresh cranberries with 1/4 cup light brown sugar on a sheet pan and roast at 375°F (190°C) for 20 minutes or until golden and caramelized. Cool. Prepare the basic ice cream, substituting the cranberries for the blueberries.

raspberry & hazelnut muffin ice cream
Prepare the basic ice cream, substituting raspberry muffins for the blueberry muffins and 1/4 cup crushed toasted or roasted hazelnuts for the fresh blueberries.

chocolate & apple muffin ice cream
Prepare the basic ice cream, substituting chocolate muffins for the blueberry muffins and 1 peeled, cored, and chopped eating apple for the blueberries.

gelato favorites

Gelato is the Italian name for a rich, smooth ice, usually enriched with egg yolks stirred into a custard base. Fresh fruits, fruit purées, and other favorite flavors can all be added or swirled through. Because gelato contains raw eggs, warn any guests who might prefer not to eat them. For the same reason, gelato should not be stored for more than a month. But I doubt it will last that long!

gelato di crema

see variations page 66

This simplest of Italian ice creams is made with a cooked egg custard and cream and can be used as the basis for almost all other gelato flavors. It is also delicious just on its own.

2 1/2 cups light cream
5 egg yolks
1/2 cup superfine sugar

Heat the cream until it is beginning to bubble, then cool slightly.

In a large heatproof bowl, beat the egg yolks and sugar until thick and creamy. Beat the cooling cream gently into the eggs.

Put the bowl over a pan of gently simmering water and stir with a wooden spoon until the custard just coats the back of the spoon. Remove the bowl and let it cool.

When the custard is completely cooled, pour into an ice cream maker and process according to the manufacturer's directions or use the hand-mixing method (page 8). Stop churning when it is almost firm, transfer to a freezer container, and leave in the freezer for 15 minutes before serving, or until required.

This gelato is best eaten fresh, but it can be frozen for up to 1 month. Take out at least 15 minutes before serving to soften slightly.

Makes about 1 1/4 pints

strawberry gelato

see variations page 67

When made with really sweet, ripe strawberries, this gelato is sure to bring back happy memories of childhood. Enjoy it simply on its own.

1 recipe gelato di crema (page 49)
3 1/2 cups hulled and chopped
   fresh strawberries

2 tbsp. superfine sugar
1 tsp. lemon juice
1 tsp. pure vanilla extract

Prepare the basic gelato recipe (or one of its variations) and let cool completely.

Purée the strawberries in a blender or food processor with the sugar, lemon juice, and vanilla extract. Pour through a fine-mesh strainer to remove seeds, if desired.

Stir the strawberry purée into the basic gelato until well blended. Pour into an ice cream maker and process according to the manufacturer's directions or into a freezer container and use the hand-mixing method (page 8). Stop churning when it is almost firm, transfer to a freezer container, and leave in the freezer for 15 minutes before serving, or until required.

This gelato is best eaten within 1 month. Take out 15 minutes before serving to soften.

Makes about 2 3/4 pints

luxury vanilla gelato

see variations page 68

The very best, warm vanilla flavor is acquired by steeping a vanilla bean in warm milk and then scraping out the tiny black seeds from inside the bean. The seeds give a lovely appearance to the gelato, too.

1 1/4 cups whole milk
1 vanilla bean
6 egg yolks

1/2 cup superfine sugar
1 1/4 cups heavy cream, whipped

Heat the milk and vanilla bean to scalding, remove from the heat, and let steep for about 10 minutes. Remove the vanilla bean, wipe dry, and make a slit down one side with a sharp knife. Open the bean and with a long thin knife, scrape the tiny black seeds into the milk.

In a large heatproof bowl, whisk the egg yolks and sugar together until thick and creamy. Whisk in the warm milk and then place the bowl over a pan of simmering water and stir with a wooden spoon until the custard thickens enough to coat the back of the spoon. Cool.

When completely cooled, fold in the whipped cream. Pour into an ice cream maker and process according to the manufacturer's instructions, or hand mix (page 8). Stop churning when it is almost firm, transfer to a freezer container, and leave in the freezer for 15 minutes before serving, or until required. This gelato is best eaten soon, but it can be frozen for up to a month. Take out 15 minutes before serving to soften slightly.

Makes about 1 1/4 pints

pistachio gelato

see variations page 69

This really is a nut lover's dream gelato, especially if you make the walnut variation.

2 cups shelled pistachios
a few drops of pure almond extract
a few drops of pure vanilla extract
1 recipe gelato di crema (page 49)

Soak the shelled pistachios in boiling water for 5 minutes, then drain and rub off the skins with a clean cloth. Grind the nuts to a paste in a blender or food processor with a few drops each of almond and vanilla extract, adding just a very little hot water to help create a smooth purée.

Prepare the basic gelato or one of its variations. Stir the purée into the gelato, taste, and add a few more drops of either or both extracts, if necessary, to taste.

Pour into an ice cream maker and process according to the manufacturer's directions or into a freezer container and use the hand-mixing method (page 8). Stop churning when it is almost firm, transfer to a freezer container, and leave in the freezer for 15 minutes before serving, or until required.

A rich nut ice cream like this should not be frozen for more than a couple of weeks. Take it out of the freezer 15 minutes before serving to soften slightly.

Makes about 1 1/2 pints

bitter chocolate gelato

see variations page 70

Just as a good chocolate ice cream should be — dark, bitter, and smooth!

2 1/2 cups whole milk
7 oz. dark chocolate, broken into pieces
5 egg yolks

1/4 cup light brown sugar
1 cup heavy cream, whipped

Heat half the milk in a pan with the chocolate until melted and smooth, stirring occasionally. Set aside to cool. Bring the rest of the milk to almost boiling. In a large heatproof bowl, whisk the egg yolks and sugar until thick, then gradually whisk in the hot milk. Place the bowl over a pan of simmering water and stir with a wooden spoon until the custard just coats the back of the spoon. Remove from the heat and set aside to cool completely.

When cooled, blend the custard and chocolate milk together, then fold in the whipped cream. Pour into an ice cream maker and process according to the manufacturer's directions or pour into a freezer container and use the hand-mixing method (page 8). Churn for only 15 to 20 minutes or until firm. Transfer to the freezer and freeze for 15 minutes before serving or until required.

This densely textured gelato is best eaten fresh, but it can be frozen for up to 1 month. Take out at least 15 minutes before serving to soften slightly.

Makes about 2 1/2 pints

raspberry ripple gelato

see variations page 71

When raspberries are at their best, enjoy this brightly colored ice cream bursting with
fresh sweet flavor.

4 cups fresh raspberries
1/4 cup superfine sugar
1 tsp. lemon juice
1 recipe gelato di crema (page 49)

Take out 1/4 cup of raspberries and crush briefly. Set aside. Mix together the remaining
berries, the sugar, and the lemon juice. Press through a sieve. Set aside 4 tablespoons of
the purée to chill.

Prepare the basic gelato di crema recipe. Fold the raspberry purée into the cooled custard.
Churn or freeze as before until nearly firm.

Transfer the gelato to an airtight freezer container and add alternating spoonfuls of the
reserved fruit purée and the crushed raspberries, so that the mixture will ripple as you serve
it. Freeze for 15 minutes or until required.

This gelato can be frozen for about 1 month. Remove from the freezer at least 15 minutes
before serving to soften, because the whole fruits can make it difficult to serve.

Makes about 1 1/4 pints

lemon gelato

see variations page 72

This is a delicately lemon-flavored gelato, perfect to enjoy with fresh fruits. (The photo shows the lemon & mint variation given on page 72.)

1 recipe light gelato (page 66)
2 unwaxed lemons

Prepare the basic light gelato and then blend in the finely grated zest of the lemons and at least 1/2 cup lemon juice.

Pour into an ice cream maker and process according to the manufacturer's instructions, or use the hand-mixing method (page 8). Stop churning when it is almost firm, transfer to a freezer container, and leave in the freezer for 15 minutes before serving, or until required.

This gelato is best eaten fresh, but it can be frozen for up to 1 month. Take out of the freezer 15 minutes before serving to soften slightly.

Makes about 1 1/4 pints

tutti-frutti gelato

see variations page 73

Add a riot of colors and flavors to a simple gelato and create your own masterpiece.

1 recipe gelato di crema (page 49)
1 cup chopped candied, crystallized, or glacéed fruits
    (cherries, pineapple, citrus peel, ginger)

Prepare the basic gelato and churn until partly frozen. Mix in your preferred fruits and freeze until required.

Although best eaten fresh, this gelato can be frozen for up to 1 month. Take out of the freezer 15 minutes before serving to soften slightly.

Makes about 1 1/2 pints

coffee gelato

see variations page 74

This is the perfect after-dinner ice cream with a little whipped cream and perhaps a dash of liqueur poured over!

1 1/4 cups light cream
5 egg yolks
1/2 cup superfine sugar

1 tsp. pure vanilla extract
1 1/4 cups freshly brewed extra-strong espresso

Heat the cream until just beginning to bubble, then cool slightly.

In a large heatproof bowl, beat the egg yolks, sugar, and vanilla until thick and creamy. Whisk in the hot cream and coffee, and then place the bowl over a pan of gently simmering water. Stir constantly with a wooden spoon until the custard just coats the back of the spoon.

Remove the bowl from the heat and let cool. When completely cooled, pour into an ice cream maker and process according to the manufacturer's directions, or use the hand-mixing method (page 8). Stop churning when it is almost firm, transfer to a freezer container, and leave in the freezer for 15 minutes before serving, or until required.

This gelato is delicious fresh, but it can be frozen for up to 3 months. Take out 15 minutes before serving to soften slightly.

Makes about 1 1/4 pints

kumquat gelato

see variations page 75

Adding this sweet and sticky, marmalade-style citrus fruit gives an unusual thickness to the ice cream.

2 cups sliced kumquats
2 tbsp. dark rum or orange juice
3 tbsp. light brown sugar

2 to 3 tbsp. hot water
1 recipe gelato di crema (page 49)

Cook the kumquats in a small pan with the rum, brown sugar, and hot water. Allow them to bubble gently until they turn golden and syrupy. Remove from heat. Put aside 2 tablespoons of the fruit in syrup if you wish to decorate the gelato with it. Cool.

Prepare the basic gelato and stir in the cooled fruit before churning. This mixture will take only about half the usual freezing time.

Top with the reserved fruit when serving.

This ice cream can be stored for up to 1 month in the freezer. Remember to take it out 15 minutes before serving to allow it to soften slightly.

Makes about 1 1/2 pints

variations

gelato di crema

see base recipe page 49

light gelato
Prepare the basic recipe, substituting whole milk for the light cream.

half & half gelato
Prepare the basic recipe, substituting half low-fat milk and half heavy cream for the light cream.

buttermilk gelato
Use buttermilk instead of the cream when preparing the basic recipe.

very rich gelato with ginger
Prepare the basic recipe, using heavy cream instead of light cream, and adding 2 tablespoons stem ginger syrup. When almost firm, stir in 6 preserved stem gingers, roughly chopped.

clotted cream gelato
When halfway through churning or freezing the basic recipe, blend in 1 cup softened clotted cream.

strawberry gelato

see base recipe page 50

crushed strawberries & cream gelato

Prepare the basic gelato di crema. Crush 3 1/2 cups strawberries with a fork and stir into the gelato along with 1 cup sweetened whipped cream. Leave the mixtures well swirled and unblended.

strawberry & orange gelato

Prepare the basic gelato di crema, adding the finely grated zest of 2 oranges and replacing some of the light cream with the juice of 1 orange. Then combine with the strawberry purée and continue as usual.

fraise gelato

Prepare the basic recipe, adding 4 to 6 tablespoons Fraise to the strawberries before puréeing.

strawberry mallow ice

Prepare the basic strawberry gelato, stirring in 1 cup mini-marshmallows or chopped large marshmallows just before the final freezing.

variations

luxury vanilla gelato

see base recipe page 53

stracciatella gelato
Prepare the basic recipe, stirring in 3/4 cup dark chocolate shavings or flakes when it is almost frozen.

cinnamon & prune gelato
Prepare the basic recipe, adding 1 teaspoon ground cinnamon to the milk. When the gelato is almost frozen, stir in 3/4 cup pitted prunes that you have poached in a little water until soft, cooled, and puréed.

christmas marrons glacés gelato
Prepare the basic recipe, adding 4 tablespoons brandy, and churn until almost firm. Stir in 1/2 cup chopped marrons glacés (candied chestnuts).

gooseberry crush gelato
Cook 3 cups gooseberries with 1/4 cup superfine sugar. Purée, strain, and cool. Stir the purée into the partly frozen gelato. Continue churning until firm.

rhubarb fool gelato
Cook 3 cups chopped rhubarb with 1/4 cup superfine sugar (or more to taste) and 2 tablespoons water. Purée, strain, and cool. Stir the rhubarb purée and 2 stiffly whipped egg whites into the gelato when it is partly frozen, then continue freezing as in the base recipe.

variations

pistachio gelato

see base recipe page 54

crunchy roasted pistachio gelato
Roast 1 cup shelled pistachio nuts until they smell wonderful and begin to change color. Roughly chop, then let cool completely. Prepare the basic pistachio gelato, stirring in the roasted nuts just before it is fully frozen.

walnut & pistachio gelato
Prepare the basic recipe, stirring in 1/2 cup roasted, cooled, and chopped walnuts before it is fully frozen.

honey & yogurt pistachio gelato
Replace 1/2 cup of the light cream of basic recipe with 3 tablespoons clear honey and 1 cup thick Greek yogurt.

pomegranate pistachio gelato
Prepare the basic recipe, stirring in 1/2 cup roasted and cooled pomegranate seeds before it is fully frozen. Serve drizzled with pomegranate syrup.

pistachio halva gelato
Prepare the basic recipe, stirring in 1/2 cup crumbled pistachio halva just before the final freezing.

variations

bitter chocolate gelato

see base recipe page 57

bailey's mint chocolate gelato
Prepare the basic recipe, replacing half the heavy cream with 1/2 cup Bailey's mint chocolate Irish cream liqueur.

white chocolate swirl gelato
Just before the final freezing, stir 3 ounces melted white chocolate briefly through the dark ice cream.

praline rum truffle gelato
Prepare the basic recipe, adding 4 tablespoons rum with the whipped cream. Just before freezing, stir in 3 tablespoons crushed praline (page 14).

tiramisu gelato
Replace the whipped cream of the basic recipe with mascarpone.
Just before the final freezing, lightly stir in 12 ladyfingers previously soaked in 2 to 3 tablespoons coffee liqueur.

chocolate gelato with raspberry ripple
Prepare the basic recipe, but just before the final freezing, briefly stir through 1 cup raspberries puréed with 1 tablespoon superfine sugar and strained.

raspberry ripple gelato

see base recipe page 58

raspberry-ricotta ripple gelato

Blend 1/2 cup ricotta with 1 tablespoon lemon juice, 1 tablespoon superfine sugar, and 1 tablespoon milk until smooth. Prepare the basic recipe, (omitting the 1/4 cup crushed berries) and when swirling in the raspberry purée, also very lightly stir in the ricotta.

raspberry-meringue ripple gelato

Prepare the basic recipe. When finished churning, stir in 1/2 cup crumbled meringues along with the reserved purée and crushed berries.

raspberry-white chocolate ripple gelato

Prepare the basic recipe, freezing until almost firm, then stir in 1/4 cup white chocolate chips or chunks before adding the raspberry sauce and crushed berries.

black cherry & raspberry ripple gelato

Cook 1/2 cup pitted and chopped black cherries with 1/8 cup superfine sugar and 2 teaspoons lemon juice. Purée, strain, and cool. Prepare the basic gelato, using only 3 1/2 cups raspberries, 1/8 cup sugar, and a little lemon juice. When almost frozen, lightly stir in the cherry purée, and freeze until you are ready to serve.

variations

lemon gelato

see base recipe page 61

lemon & mint gelato
Prepare the basic recipe, adding 3 tablespoons finely chopped fresh mint before churning.

lime gelato
Replace the lemon in the basic recipe with lime.

blood orange gelato
Prepare the base recipe, replacing the lemons with 1 or 2 blood oranges (depending on how much juice they have).

limoncello gelato
Prepare the basic recipe, replacing one of the lemons with 6 tablespoons limoncello.

lemon gelato with black currant ripple
Prepare the basic recipe. When spooning into a freezer container, ripple in 3 to 4 tablespoons softened black currant jam or jelly.

variations

tutti-frutti gelato

see base recipe page 62

nutty tutti-frutti gelato
Prepare the basic recipe, freezing until nearly firm. Stir in 1/4 cup chopped pistachios, walnuts, or pecans along with the candied fruits.

tropical tutti-frutti gelato
Prepare the basic recipe, substituting dried tropical fruits such as banana, mango, papaya, and pineapple for the candied fruits.

fruit salad tutti-frutti gelato
Prepare the basic recipe, substituting fresh crisp fruits (apple, plum, pear, grapes, and cherries) for the candied fruits. This version is best eaten within a few hours before the fruits become too icy hard.

fig & honey tutti-frutti gelato
Chop 1/2 cup dried figs and mix with 2 tablespoons warmed honey. Leave for 10 minutes. Prepare the basic recipe with no fruit until almost firm, then stir in the figs and honey and freeze as normal.

christmas tutti-frutti gelato
Mix 3/4 cup chopped dried fruits with 4 tablespoons brandy or rum; let steep for 1 hour. Prepare the basic recipe, replacing the candied fruits with the dried fruit in brandy.

variations

coffee gelato

see base recipe page 63

caramel & walnut coffee crema
Prepare the basic recipe, adding 6 tablespoons toffee sauce (page 13). When transferring to a freezer container, stir in 1/2 cup roasted, cooled, and roughly chopped walnuts.

coffee cream ripple gelato
When transferring the basic recipe to a freezer container, stir in 4 tablespoons coffee liqueur.

irish coffee gelato
Prepare the basic recipe, adding 4 to 5 tablespoons whiskey. When transferring to a freezer container, gently fold in 1/2 cup thickly whipped but not stiff heavy cream.

mocha latte gelato
Prepare the basic ice cream, using 1 1/2 times as much cream and only half the espresso, and adding 1 tablespoon sifted cocoa powder to the hot cream. Serve sprinkled with cocoa powder.

variations

kumquat gelato

see base recipe page 64

tangerine gelato
Prepare the basic recipe, replacing the kumquats with peeled and sliced tangerines.

kumquat & grand marnier gelato
Add 4 to 6 tablespoons Grand Marnier to the basic recipe.

kumquat & coconut gelato
Prepare the basic recipe. Stir 1 cup shredded, toasted, and cooled coconut into the gelato when it is almost frozen.

kumquat & macaroon gelato
Stir in 1 cup crumbled macaroons when the basic recipe is almost firm.

kumquat & cookies gelato
Prepare the basic recipe, stirring in 1/2 cup crumbled chocolate cookies just before the final freezing.

sorbets

Cool and refreshing sorbets can make the perfect

end to a meal or a delicious palate cleanser in the

midst of a rich dinner. To best enjoy their crisp

texture, they should be eaten within a few hours of

being made. Any flavored or fruit syrup can be

quickly turned into a sorbet, so once you have made

a few of these, try your hand at your own creations.

lemon sorbet

see variations page 90

This sharp, fresh sorbet is perfect to serve as a palate cleanser or, with more sugar to taste, as a crisp, refreshing dessert.

2 large juicy unwaxed lemons, washed
1/2 cup superfine sugar
1 1/2 cups boiling water

Finely grate the zest of the lemons into a bowl. Squeeze the lemon juice (at least 3/4 cup) into the bowl and add the sugar and water. Stir well and leave for 1 to 2 hours in a cool place, stirring occasionally, until the sugar has dissolved. Chill.

Pour the mixture into an ice cream maker and process according to the manufacturer's directions, or pour it into a freezer container and freeze following the hand-mixing method (page 8).

When the sorbet is firm, freeze it in a freezer container for 15 to 20 minutes or until ready to serve. If necessary, transfer it to the refrigerator 10 minutes before serving to soften.

This sorbet will not be good if frozen for longer than 2 to 3 weeks.

Makes about 1 pint

strawberry sorbet

see variations page 91

Few sorbets are as refreshing as this light and summery version.

1 cup vanilla sugar syrup (page 12)
2 tbsp. lemon or lime juice
juice and zest of 1 orange
3 1/2 cups fresh, hulled strawberries

Combine the sugar syrup, citrus juices, and orange zest. Chill.

Purée and strain the strawberries, and mix with the cold syrup. Pour into an ice cream maker and process according to the manufacturer's instructions, or pour into a freezer container and freeze using the hand-mixing method described on page 8.

When the sorbet is firm, freeze it in a freezer container for 15 to 20 minutes or until ready to serve. If necessary, remove it from the freezer 5 to 10 minutes before serving to soften.

This sorbet can be frozen for up to 1 month, but it is best eaten as soon as possible.

Makes about 1 3/4 pints

refreshing lime sorbet

see variations page 92

The vibrant fragrance of fresh lime is wonderful in this sorbet, especially if it's served in lime shells. Try to find the softest, juiciest limes.

6 unwaxed dark green juicy limes
1 to 1 1/4 cups superfine sugar
1 cup water
lime or mint leaves, to garnish

Finely grate the zest of 2 limes into a bowl, then add the juice of all the limes. Add the sugar and water to the bowl and let stand for 1 to 2 hours in a cool place, stirring occasionally, until the sugar has dissolved. Pour the mixture into an ice cream maker and process according to the manufacturer's instructions, or hand-mix (page 8).

When it is firm, freeze it in a freezer container for 15 minutes or up to several hours before serving. If you freeze it for longer, remove it from the freezer 10 minutes before serving to soften. This sorbet can be frozen for up to 3 weeks, but it is best eaten as soon as possible.

This recipe makes enough sorbet to fill 10 lime shells. To serve this way, neatly remove the top third of the limes and squeeze out their juice into a bowl with a reamer or hand juicer, taking care not to split the shells. Scoop out and discard any remaining pulp. Spoon the sorbet into the shells and freeze until serving. Add a lime or mint leaf to garnish each filled lime shell.

Makes about 1 pint

mango sorbet

see variations page 93

Mango makes the easiest and most delicious sorbet, with a velvety smooth consistency.
If you can ever find Indian mangoes (smaller and yellower), try them; their flavor is even
better and they are amazingly perfumed.

juice of 1 lemon
juice of 1/2 orange
1/2 cup superfine sugar
2 large ripe mangoes
1 large egg white, whisked

Mix the fruit juices with the sugar. Peel and pit the mangoes, then reduce the flesh to a
purée in a blender. Transfer to a large bowl and stir in the fruit juice. Fold in the whisked
egg white.

Pour into an ice cream maker and process according to the manufacturer's instructions,
or pour into a freezer container and freeze using the hand-mixing method (page 8).

When the sorbet is firm, freeze it in a freezer container for 15 minutes or until ready to
serve. If necessary, remove it from the freezer 5 to 10 minutes before serving to soften.
Serve on its own or with a few mango slices and some raspberry sauce (page 14).

This sorbet is best eaten fresh, but it can be frozen for up to 1 month.

Makes about 1 pint

pear sorbet

see variations page 94

The delicate flavor of pears is best appreciated when they are perfectly ripe, so be sure to choose the very best fruit.

4 large (about 2 lbs.) ripe, but not soft, Comice or Bartlett pears
juice of 1 small lemon
1 cup sugar syrup (page 11), chilled
1 medium egg white

Peel and core the fruit. Purée in a blender along with the lemon juice. Pour straight into the syrup to avoid any discoloration.

Pour into an ice cream maker and process according to the manufacturer's instructions, or pour into a freezer container and freeze using the hand-mixing method on page 8.

When the sorbet just starts to turn slushy, lightly whisk the egg white until frothy. Add it to the sorbet and continue churning or freezing until firm. Leave the sorbet in the freezer for 15 minutes or until required. If necessary, remove it from the freezer just 5 to 10 minutes before serving to soften.

Pear sorbet is best eaten as soon as possible or within a few days.

Makes about 1 1/4 pints

ruby grapefruit sorbet

see variations page 95

Serve this lovely pink sorbet in grapefruit shells if you wish, or in tall glasses with other fresh fruits.

2 ripe ruby-red or pink grapefruits
1 cup sugar syrup (page 11)
4 tbsp. raspberry or cranberry juice

Cut the grapefruits in half. Squeeze out all the juice (taking care with the shells if you wish to serve the sorbet in them) and mix with the syrup and juice. Carefully remove and discard any remaining pulp in the shells.

Pour the mixture into an ice cream maker and process according to the manufacturer's instructions, or pour into a freezer container and freeze using the hand-mixing method (page 8).

When the sorbet is firm, spoon it into the grapefruit shells (if using) or a freezer container and freeze for 15 minutes or until ready to serve. If necessary, remove it from the freezer 5 minutes before serving to soften. Cut the grapefruit halves into wedges to serve.

This sorbet is best eaten as soon as possible, but it can be frozen for up to 3 weeks.

Makes about 1 pint

champagne cocktail sorbet

see variations page 96

Champagne is wonderful for a very special occasion, but a good dry Cava or Asti also makes an excellent sorbet. This is a very crisp and crumbly sorbet, so serve it in well-chilled glasses straight from the freezer.

1 1/2 cups water, chilled
1/2 cup grapefruit juice
1 cup superfine sugar

1 1/2 cups champagne or sparkling
  dry white wine, chilled
1 medium egg white

Mix the water, grapefruit juice, and sugar together. Chill until the sugar has dissolved. Stir in the champagne or sparkling wine. Pour into an ice cream maker and process according to the manufacturer's instructions, or into a freezer container and freeze using the hand-mixing method (page 8). Churn until it becomes slushy.

Whisk the egg white until it forms soft peaks. Add it to the bowl of sorbet while churning, or fold into the mixture in the freezer container. Continue until firm. Freeze for at least 20 minutes to firm up before serving. Serve the sorbet directly from the freezer, because it melts very quickly.

Before serving, freeze the glasses briefly, with a drop of brandy, Cassis, or Fraise in the base.

Do not keep for longer than a few days.

Makes about 2 pints

jasmine tea sorbet

see variations page 97

Tea sorbets are generally very delicate and subtle. Be careful not to oversweeten or let the tea brew for too long.

1 1/4 cups jasmine tea, chilled
1/4 cup sugar syrup (page 11), chilled
1 to 2 tsp. lemon juice
1 medium egg white

Mix together the tea, sugar syrup, and lemon juice. Pour into an ice cream maker and process according to the manufacturer's instructions, or pour into a freezer container and freeze using the hand-mixing method (page 8). Churn until slushy.

Whisk the egg white until soft peaks form, then fold into the sorbet. Continue churning and freezing until firm. Freeze for 15 minutes before serving or until required.

This sorbet has a very delicate flavor and is best eaten within 24 hours. Serve with crisp almond cookies or tuiles.

Makes just less than 1 pint

variations

lemon sorbet

see base recipe page 77

herb & lemon sorbet
To serve during dinner, prepare the basic recipe, adding 2 tablespoons finely chopped basil, mint, or dill before freezing.

sweet lemon sorbet
For dessert eating, prepare the basic recipe, adding 1/3 to 1/2 cup more superfine sugar or to taste.

lemon & lavender sorbet
Prepare the basic recipe, replacing the water with a lavender water. To make it, place 2 heaping tablespoons lavender heads in 1 cup boiling water, bring back to a boil, and turn off the heat. Let stand to infuse for 2 to 4 hours, stirring occasionally.

citrus sorbet
Prepare the basic recipe, using equal quantities of a mixture of citrus fruits.

lemon & vodka sorbet
Prepare the basic recipe, replacing 4 tablespoons of the juice with vodka.

variations

strawberry sorbet

see base recipe page 78

strawberry & drambuie sorbet
Replace the orange juice of the basic recipe with Drambuie and the orange
zest with 2 tablespoons chopped fresh lemon balm.

strawberry sorbet with balsamic vinegar & chile
Prepare the basic recipe, substituting a chile-flavored syrup (page 12) for the
vanilla syrup and balsamic vinegar for the lemon or lime juice.

strawberry sorbet with marmalade ripple
Prepare the basic recipe. When transferring the sorbet to the freezer
container for its final freezing, add 4 to 5 tablespoons softened, fine-shred
marmalade. Don't stir it through very much, but let it freeze briefly so it will
ripple when you scoop out the sorbet.

strawberry & blackberry sorbet
Prepare the basic recipe, replacing half the strawberries with the same
quantity of blackberries.

variations

refreshing lime sorbet

see base recipe page 81

lime & lychee sorbet
Purée 2 cups canned or peeled and pitted fresh lychees. Prepare half of the
basic recipe and stir in the lychee purée before churning.

lime, lemongrass & coconut sorbet
Add 1 bruised lemongrass stalk to the sugar, water, and lime mixture and let
it steep for several hours. Remove the lemongrass and add 1 cup coconut
milk. Fill the ice cream maker and proceed as directed in the basic recipe.

gin & tonic lime sorbet
Prepare the basic recipe, replacing the water with tonic water, reducing the
sugar by half, and adding 6 tablespoons gin. Serve with a slice of lime.

lime & tequila sorbet
Serve the basic recipe sorbet in cocktail glasses with salted rims and a shot
of tequila poured over.

mango sorbet

see base recipe page 82

mango & banana sorbet
Prepare the basic recipe, replacing 1 mango with 2 small ripe bananas.

mango & raspberry sorbet
Prepare the basic recipe and replace 1 mango with 2 cups mashed
raspberries (sieved if you wish).

mango & tangerine sorbet
Replace the orange and lemon juices of the basic recipe with the juice of
4 tangerines.

mango & pineapple sorbet
When preparing the basic recipe, replace 1 mango with 2 cups mashed ripe
pineapple.

mango & rum sorbet
Prepare the basic recipe and replace the lemon juice with rum.

variations

pear sorbet

see base recipe page 83

pear & quince jelly sorbet
Prepare the basic recipe, stirring in 6 tablespoons quince jelly just
before freezing.

pear & licorice sorbet with pastis chaser
Make the sugar syrup with 2 sticks licorice and let them
dissolve. Continue with the basic recipe, but omit the egg white. Serve
with a shot or chaser of pastis or your favorite anise liqueur.

pear turkish delight sorbet
Prepare the basic recipe, substituting 1/2 cup rose water for the lemon juice.
Churn until almost firm and then stir in 1/2 cup chopped Turkish delight candy.

pear & chocolate sorbet
Prepare the basic recipe, stirring in 1/4 cup grated dark chocolate when
it is almost firm. Serve with hot chocolate sauce (page 13).

pear sorbet with cardamom & poppy seeds
When making the sugar syrup, flavor it with 6 cracked cardamom pods,
and let cool. Strain and then stir in 3 tablespoons poppy seeds. Continue
with the basic recipe.

variations

ruby grapefruit sorbet

see base recipe page 84

blood orange sorbet
Prepare the basic recipe, but replace the grapefruit with blood oranges. Taste, and stir in more sugar if needed.

grand marnier sorbet
Prepare the basic recipe, but replace the raspberry or cranberry juice with Grand Marnier or Cointreau.

grapefruit & pineapple sorbet
Stir in 3/4 cup mashed pineapple halfway through churning and mixing the basic recipe.

grapefruit & papaya sorbet
Prepare the basic recipe, but stir in 3/4 cup mashed papaya halfway through churning and mixing.

grapefruit & cranberry sorbet
Prepare the basic recipe, stirring in 1/2 cup cooked and puréed cranberries and adding extra sugar to taste.

variations

champagne cocktail sorbet

see base recipe page 87

cider cocktail sorbet
Replace the champagne of the basic recipe with the same amount of dry cider. Serve with a shot of Calvados and apple slices.

summer punch sorbet
Prepare the basic recipe, replacing the champagne with 1/2 cup Pimm's diluted with 1/2 cup lemonade and 1/2 cup ginger ale. Top with a sprig of mint or borage.

bloody mary sorbet
Prepare the basic recipe, replacing the champagne with tomato juice and using lemon instead of grapefruit juice. Add salt, black pepper, and Worcestershire sauce to taste and serve with a shot of vodka or dry sherry.

elderflower cocktail sorbet
Prepare the base recipe, replacing the champagne with nonalcoholic elderflower champagne.

variations

jasmine tea sorbet

see base recipe page 88

green tea sorbet
Use green tea instead of jasmine tea, and add extra sugar to taste.

earl grey tea sorbet
Prepare the basic recipe, using Earl Grey tea instead of jasmine tea. Serve with lemon slices.

iced jagger tea sorbet
Prepare the basic recipe, using Indian or breakfast tea instead of jasmine tea, and adding 4 tablespoons schnapps. Serve with a chaser of schnapps.

chamomile tea sorbet
Prepare the basic recipe, using chamomile tea instead of jasmine tea, and adding extra lemon juice to taste.

mint tea sorbet
Try replacing the jasmine tea with mint tea.

granitas &
water ices

Water ices and granitas are meant to be crumbly

and crystallized, unlike the smoother sorbets. Catch

them at the stage when they are almost hard, use a

fork to break the ice into crystals, serve before they

melt, and eat as soon as possible.

watermelon granita

see variations page 118

Be sure to find the ripest watermelon so that it has the most flavor.

3 cups watermelon purée (approximately
   1 3/4-lb. piece)
1/2 cup superfine sugar

2 tsp. pure vanilla extract
juice of 1 pink or red grapefruit

Mix the watermelon purée with the other ingredients. Chill for 1 to 2 hours, stirring occasionally to make sure the sugar dissolves.

Pour into a freezer container and freeze until almost firm. Stir with a fork to break into crystals. Put back into the freezer and refreeze again until almost firm. Remove, break into nice, even crystals, and serve in pretty cocktail glasses.

Makes about 1 1/4 pints

green mint granita

see variations page 119

This wonderfully aromatic water ice is delicious after spicy dishes as a palate cleanser or as a refreshing slushy drink on a hot day. Or serve it as an after-dinner frappé.

1 1/2 cups (12 fl oz) boiling water
8 sprigs fresh mint (preferably picked early in
   the day or used immediately after buying)
3/4 cup superfine sugar

1 1/2 cups ice water
2 tbsp. finely chopped fresh mint leaves
green food coloring (optional)
mint sprigs for garnish (optional)

Pour the boiling water onto the mint sprigs and sugar in a bowl and let cool, stirring occasionally. Add the ice water and chill.

Strain the liquid into a freezer container and stir in the chopped mint (add a few drops of green food coloring if you wish). Freeze until partly frozen, then stir with a fork to break into crystals. Return to the freezer and refreeze until almost firm. Remove and stir with a fork to break into nice, even crystals.

Serve in iced tall glasses, with more sprigs of mint if desired.

Makes about 1 1/4 pints

coffee granita

see variations page 120

This is a strong black coffee water ice tempered with a little sweetness and topped with a swirl of nutty cream.

3 cups freshly made very strong black coffee
1/3 cup superfine sugar
1/4 tsp. pure vanilla extract

1 cup water, chilled
1 cup whipping cream
2 tbsp. toasted hazelnuts

Mix the hot coffee, sugar, and vanilla together. Let cool, stirring occasionally until the sugar has dissolved. Add the chilled water and pour into a freezer container.

Freeze until slushy. Lightly break up with a fork, then continue freezing until almost firm.

Finely grind most of the nuts and roughly crush the rest. Whip the cream until frothy and fold in the ground nuts. Place in the freezer for the last 15 minutes before serving.

Chill 4 to 6 tall glasses. Remove the granita from the freezer and break it up with a fork. Fill the chilled glasses with the coffee ice crystals. Top with a swirl of the iced cream and sprinkle on a few of the crushed nuts. Refreeze no longer than an hour, then serve directly from the freezer.

Makes about 1 1/2 pints

summer berry water ice

see variations page 121

A mixture of really ripe berries gives a luscious flavor of summer and a gorgeous splash of color.

1/3 to 1/2 cup superfine sugar (depending on ripeness and mix of berries)
1 cup water

2 cups fresh berries
1 tbsp. lemon juice

Mix the sugar and water in a pan and bring to a boil, stirring occasionally. Immediately remove from the heat.

Pick over or hull the fruit as needed, wash and dry, and add to the pan of sugar water. Stir to make sure the sugar is dissolved and leave in the hot syrup until the fruit softens.

Cool slightly, add the lemon juice, and then purée, or push through a fine-mesh sieve if you want a smooth purée. Pour into a freezer container. Freeze until partly frozen, break up with a fork into crystals, then freeze again until almost frozen, whisking gently once more during this time.

To serve, break up the granita into crystals and serve with more berries or chewy meringues.

Makes about 1 3/4 pints

lavender granita

see variations page 122

Pretty pink-purple lavender heads produce this stunning water ice with a most delicately perfumed taste.

2 tbsp. fresh lavender heads
1/2 cup superfine sugar
1 cup boiling water

1 cup chilled water
2 tsp. lemon juice
2 tsp. orange juice

Place the lavender heads and sugar in a bowl and add the boiling water. Stir well, then cover and let cool completely.

Strain, then add the chilled water and fruit juices. Pour into a freezer container and freeze until almost firm, breaking up with a fork once during freezing. Just before serving, break up again with a fork into nice, even crystals.

The flavor of this delicate ice will soon disappear, so eat it as soon as possible.

Makes about 1 pint

dark chocolate granita

see variations page 123

If you have not tried a chocolate water ice before, you are in for a treat! It is like eating a frozen bar of crumbled chocolate — definitely for chocoholics.

2 1/2 cups water
3/4 cup dark brown sugar
1/2 cup unsweetened cocoa powder, sifted

3 tbsp. light corn syrup
1/2 cup white chocolate, flaked, grated, or
    finely chopped, plus more for decoration

Gently warm the water, brown sugar, cocoa, and corn syrup together until blended. Stir gently until the mixture is smooth. Set aside to cool completely.

Stir in the white chocolate. Pour into a freezer container and freeze until almost firm, stirring and breaking up once during freezing. Just before serving, break up again to achieve a nice, granular consistency.

To serve, scoop into bowls and sprinkle with more white chocolate.

Makes about 1 1/2 pints

passion fruit water ice

see variations page 124

Astringent passion fruit makes a delightfuly refreshing water ice.

12 ripe passion fruit
1 cup water
3/4 cup superfine sugar

1 tbsp. orange juice
1 tsp. lemon juice

Scoop out all the fruit pulp and juice and strain into a bowl to remove the black seeds. Stir in the water, sugar, and juices. Chill for about 30 minutes while the sugar dissolves. Stir occasionally.

Pour the mixture into a freezer container and freeze until almost firm, stirring and breaking up into crystals once or twice.

When ready to serve, break up the water ice with a fork until it has a granular consistency. Serve with panna cotta or crème brulée and a little fresh passion fruit juice poured over at the last moment.

Makes about 1 1/4 pints

raspberry water ice

see variations page 125

You would never guess this water ice contains wine, but it does add an unusually full-bodied flavor.

2 cups fresh raspberries
1/2 cup light red wine
1 cup water
3/4 cup superfine sugar

In a food processor or blender, combine all the ingredients thoroughly. Pour through a fine-mesh sieve until quite smooth.

Pour the mixture into a freezer container and freeze until partly frozen. Break up into crystals once, then leave until almost frozen.

To serve, break up or scrape the water ice into crystals and spoon into iced wine glasses. Leave in the freezer no longer than an hour, until you're quite ready to eat. Serve with biscotti or simple cookies.

Makes about 1 1/2 pints

soft apricot water ice

see variations page 126

Apricots, when really ripe, can be delicately aromatic and are perfect for an elegant water ice. In winter use the dried apricot variation.

3/4 lb. very ripe apricots, pitted
1/2 cup superfine sugar
1 1/2 cups water
1/4 cup Amaretto liqueur

Put the apricots in a blender with the sugar and water. Blend to a purée, then pass through a fine-mesh sieve if you want a really smooth mixture.

Stir in the Amaretto, then pour into a container to freeze until partially frozen. Whisk or break up briefly and then return to the freezer until frozen but not hard. Break up with a fork to give a crumbly crystallized effect and serve either on its own or with grilled or poached fruit.

Makes about 1 1/4 pints

baked apple water ice

see variations page 127

Soft fluffy baked or microwaved apples make a very easy and delicious water ice. Choose apples that are sharp and become soft and fluffy on cooking.

2 medium-sized tart cooking apples (such as
    Newtown Pippin, Jonagold, or Granny Smith)
4 tbsp. honey
1 1/2 cups water
1/2 cup superfine sugar

1 tbsp. lemon juice
1/2 tsp. ground cinnamon, plus a sprinkle more
    for garnish
ginger snaps (page 17) or cookies to serve

Make cuts around the middle of the apples (so they don't split on cooking) and either microwave or bake until quite soft. Let stand until cool enough to handle, and then scoop out the fluffy white pulp into a bowl. Cool completely.

Gently stir in the honey, water, sugar, lemon juice, and 1/2 teaspoon cinnamon. Mix until well blended and the sugar has dissolved.

Pour into a freezer container and freeze until almost firm, stirring and breaking up with a fork once or twice. To serve, break up again into even crystals, then serve with ginger cookies or in ginger snaps (page 17) that you have shaped into baskets while they cool. Sprinkle with a little more cinnamon before serving.

Makes about 1 1/4 pints

variations

watermelon granita

see base recipe page 99

charentais or cantaloupe granita
Prepare the basic recipe, omitting the vanilla, using only half the sugar, and replacing the grapefruit juice with 2 tablespoons lemon juice. You will need 2 to 3 small charentais or cantaloupe melons.

kiwi granita
Prepare the basic recipe, replacing the melon purée with kiwi purée (about 12 kiwis) and replacing the grapefruit juice with 1 to 2 tablespoons lemon juice. If you like the black seeds, there is no need to strain.

watermelon & orange granita
Prepare the basic recipe, replacing the grapefruit juice with the rind and juice of 2 large oranges.

melon & papaya granita
Prepare the basic recipe, replacing half the watermelon purée with the same quantity of puréed ripe papaya.

variations

green mint granita

see base recipe page 100

crème de menthe frappé
Prepare the basic recipe, and serve in tiny iced glasses, with crème de menthe poured on top at the last minute, as an after-dinner liqueur water ice.

mint & orange granita
Prepare the basic recipe, stirring in 1 tablespoon finely grated orange zest. Serve in orange shells.

mint & chocolate granita cups
Prepare the basic recipe, stirring in 1/4 cup finely grated white chocolate. Serve in small dark chocolate cups (page 15).

pineapple mint granita
Prepare the basic recipe, using pineapple mint. Serve scooped onto thick slices of sweet pineapple.

crunchy peppermint ice
Prepare the basic recipe, stirring in 1/4 cup crushed peppermint candy before starting to freeze.

variations

coffee granita

see base recipe page 103

coffee granita with liqueur crystals
Prepare the basic recipe, omitting the nuts. Mix 6 tablespoons coffee liqueur (not a creamy one) with 6 tablespoons of the nearly frozen granita, then freeze. When ready to serve, scrape the liqueur granita into shavings. Sprinkle the crystals over the granita, which has been topped with whipped cream.

turkish coffee granita
Prepare the basic recipe, using only 1/3 of the sugar, omitting the vanilla, and adding 1/2 cup brandy.

two-tier granita
Prepare the basic recipe, but divide the sweetened coffee into two containers. Add the whipped cream without nuts to one container and whisk in. Add 1 tablespoon orange zest to the other container. Freeze both parts separately. To serve, layer the two parts in a chilled tall glass.

mexican mocha granita
Melt 2 ounces dark chocolate with 1 tablespoon light brown sugar, a pinch of cinnamon, and a shot of brandy. Cool. Prepare the basic recipe, omitting the nuts, and pouring some mocha sauce into the base of each glass. At the last moment, drizzle more sauce over the whipped cream.

variations

summer berry water ice

see base recipe page 104

black currant water ice
Prepare the basic recipe using only black currants; add extra sugar to taste.
Serve with iced Cassis or black currant liqueur poured over the top.

blueberry water ice
Prepare the basic granita recipe using only blueberries and slightly less sugar
and adding 2 tablespoons lemon juice.

cherry water ice
Prepare the basic granita recipe using ripe pitted black cherries. Serve with a
sprinkling of dark chocolate.

gooseberry water ice
Prepare the basic granita recipe using ripe gooseberries and extra sugar to
taste. You might like to add a drop of green or pink food coloring for a more
dramatic effect.

blackberry & apple water ice
Prepare the basic recipe, replacing the 2 cups of berries with 1 cup
blackberries and 1 cup peeled and chopped apple.

variations

lavender granita

see base recipe page 107

geranium granita
Prepare the basic recipe, replacing the lavender heads with 8 to 10 fresh young lemon- or rose-scented geranium leaves.

black currant leaf granita
Prepare the basic recipe, replacing the lavender with 10 to 12 fresh young black currant leaves and the orange and lemon juices with lime juice.

black currant leaf & dessert wine granita
Prepare the basic recipe, replacing the lavender with 10 to 12 black currant leaves and half the water with a sweet dessert wine.

elderflower granita
Prepare the basic recipe, using 10 to 12 elderflower blossom heads instead of the lavender.

lime blossom granita
Prepare the basic recipe, replacing the lavender with 2 to 3 teaspoons lime blossom tea leaves.

variations

dark chocolate granita

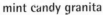
see base recipe page 108

mint candy granita
Prepare the basic granita, with or without the white chocolate. When partly
frozen break up the mixture and stir in 1 cup crushed or crumbled mint
candy bar. Freeze briefly until ready to serve.

praline crunch granita
Prepare the basic granita. When partly frozen, stir in 6 to 8 tablespoons of
roughly crushed praline (page 14).

chocolate granita with black cherries
Cook 1/2 cup pitted black cherries with 1/8 cup light brown sugar until
tender, then chill. Prepare the basic granita and serve with the cherries in
their syrup.

chocolate granita with berries
Prepare the basic granita. When partly frozen, break up the mixture and stir
in 1 cup dried cranberries, blueberries, or cherries. Freeze briefly until ready
to serve.

variations

passion fruit water ice

see base recipe page 111

passion fruit & cape gooseberry water ice
Prepare the basic granita, replacing half the passion fruit with 1 cup ripe cape gooseberries (physalis), crushed and puréed.

passion fruit & melon water ice
Prepare the basic recipe, replacing half the passion fruit with 1 cup cantaloupe melon purée.

passion fruit & mango water ice
Prepare the basic recipe, replacing half the passion fruit with 1 cup mango purée.

passion fruit & rum water ice
Prepare the basic recipe, replacing the fruit juice with 3 to 4 tablespoons light rum.

passion fruit & orange water ice
Prepare the basic recipe, replacing half the water with orange juice.

variations

raspberry water ice

see base recipe page 112

raspberry & rosé water ice
For a lighter flavor, prepare the basic recipe, replacing the red wine with rosé wine or sparkling rosé wine.

raspberry & rhubarb water ice
Prepare the basic recipe, replacing 1 cup raspberries with 1 cup roughly chopped rhubarb that you have poached in a little simmering water until just tender. Add extra sugar to taste and serve with whipped cream.

raspberry & red currant water ice
Prepare the basic recipe, replacing 1 cup raspberries with 1 cup cooked red currants. Add extra sugar to taste.

raspberry & plum water ice
Prepare the basic recipe, replacing 1 cup raspberries with 1 cup pitted and chopped sweet red plums, which you have poached in simmering water until just tender. A shot of iced schnapps or vodka would be good poured on top.

variations

soft apricot water ice

see base recipe page 115

apricot & kirsch water ice
Prepare the basic recipe, replacing the Amaretto with Kirsch.

peach or nectarine water ice
Prepare the basic recipe, replacing the apricots with 2 large ripe peeled and pitted peaches or nectarines.

pineapple water ice
Prepare the basic recipe, replacing the apricots with 2 cups grated ripe pineapple (approximately half a large pineapple) and the Amaretto with light rum or orange juice.

dried apricot & orange water ice
Prepare the basic recipe, using puréed dried apricots instead of fresh apricots. Simmer 1 cup dried apricots with 1 cup water and 1 cup orange juice until really tender, then purée in a blender.

apricot water ice with berry crush
Prepare the basic recipe, adding 1/2 cup fresh raspberries or small strawberries halfway through churning, to give a crushed effect.

variations

baked apple water ice

see base recipe page 116

apple cider water ice
Prepare the basic recipe, replacing the water with apple cider and omitting the cinnamon. Serve with a splash of Calvados.

apple & quince water ice
Prepare the basic recipe, replacing 1 apple with 1 very ripe quince. Cook the quince slowly and gently until softened, then peel, core, and purée and add to the apple. Serve the water ice with sweetened whipped cream.

apple & black currant water ice
Prepare the basic recipe, replacing 1 apple with 1 cup black currants. Cook the black currants with the sugar and water while the apple is cooking, then purée them and continue with the basic recipe, adding extra sugar to taste.

toffee apple water ice
Prepare the basic recipe until partly frozen. Meanwhile, freeze 1/2 cup (3 ounces) toffee candy. Crush the frozen toffees in a bag using a rolling pin. Break up the water ice with a fork, stir in the candy, and refreeze.

fresh & fruity frozen treats

Fresh, ripe, sweet fruits are just asking to be made into these luscious tangy iced desserts. With choices as varied as our light and fluffy apricot soufflé, sharp sweet crisp orange sherbet, melt-in-the-mouth berry semifreddo, and bananas with custard—where will you start?

summer berry semifreddo

see variations page 145

Semifreddo, as it sounds, is only partly frozen. Here you have a fabulously creamy and smooth ice-cold dessert richly flavored with fruits and liqueur.

4 large egg yolks
1 tsp. pure vanilla extract
1/2 cup superfine sugar
2 cups heavy cream

4 to 6 tbsp. brandy or kirsch
4 cups mixed small berries
3 tbsp. toasted sliced almonds
confectioners' sugar

Whisk the egg yolks in a bowl with the vanilla and sugar until really thick and creamy. In a separate bowl, beat the cream until thick. Add the liqueur and beat until thick again.

Purée or blend 2 cups of the berries, and strain in a fine-mesh sieve, if you wish.

Fold together the beaten egg yolks, the whipped cream, and the puréed berries. Fold in most of the remaining berries (save a few for serving with). Spoon into molds or pans that have been lined with plastic wrap, and freeze for 3 to 4 hours.

To serve, turn out onto plates and top with a few of the reserved berries, sliced almonds, and a sprinkling of confectioners' sugar.

Serves 4–6

iced blackberry & pear romanoff

see variations page 146

A delicious fall family dessert of blackberries, pears, whipped cream, thick yogurt, and crunchy meringues takes on a new light when slightly frozen.

1 cup sweet pear purée	finely grated zest of 1 lemon
1 cup heavy cream, whipped	1 cup roughly crumbled small meringues
1 cup thick Greek-style yogurt	1 cup sweet ripe blackberries

In a large bowl, mix together the pear purée, whipped cream, yogurt, and lemon zest. Add a little sugar to taste if you wish, or if the blackberries are not too sweet.

Now fold in the crumbled meringues and finally the blackberries, mixing as little as possible. Spoon into a deep freezer container and freeze for 1 to 2 hours. Do not stir while freezing.

To serve, gently spoon the mixture onto a serving plate with a few more berries.

Makes 2 pints

peach & passion fruit swirl ice cream

see variations page 147

This delicious soft peach ice cream has a swirl of passion fruit running through it.

1 1/4 cups heavy cream
1 tsp. pure vanilla extract
2 large eggs
1/4 cup superfine sugar or to taste
2 tsp. cornstarch

1 tbsp. water
4 large very ripe peaches
juice and finely grated zest of 1 orange
4 ripe passion fruit

In a small saucepan bring the cream and vanilla to boiling point. Remove from the heat. In a bowl, whisk the eggs and sugar until very pale and slightly thickened. Whisk a little of the cream into the eggs until well blended, then strain back into the saucepan. Blend the cornstarch with the water until smooth. Whisk it into the cream and egg mixture, and return the pan to the heat. Do not boil, but as the mix begins to thicken, stir constantly until it covers the back of a spoon. Set aside to cool, stirring occasionally.

Place the peaches in boiling water for about 1 minute or until the skins easily peel off. Blend or purée the flesh with the orange juice and zest and strain if required. Scoop the passion fruit flesh into a small bowl. Gently stir together the cooled custard and peach purée. Put into an ice cream maker and process according to the manufacturer's instructions, or use the hand-mixing method (page 8). When almost firm, transfer to a freezer container and swirl in most of the passion fruit. Freeze until firm or required. This ice cream can be frozen for up to 1 month. Allow about 15 minutes to soften before serving with a little more passion fruit poured on top.

Makes 1 1/2 pints

iced apricot soufflés

see variations page 148

The perfect end to a special dinner — these individual soufflés are almost frozen but yet soft enough to just spoon into. Serve them with a hot black currant sauce.

juice and finely grated zest of 1 orange
2 (1/4-oz.) envelopes unflavored gelatin
3 medium eggs, separated, plus 2 more whites
1/2 cup superfine sugar
1 tsp. pure vanilla extract

1 cup whipping cream
4 tbsp. Amaretto liqueur
1 cup apricot purée
3/4 cup black currants (fresh or frozen)
2 to 3 tbsp. superfine sugar

Prepare 4 ramekins by wrapping a band of waxed paper around the outside of each, coming to about 2 inches above the rims; secure with tape. Lightly grease the paper and inside of the dishes. Warm the orange juice in a small saucepan, sprinkle on the gelatin, and let dissolve. Cool. Put the orange zest, yolks, sugar, and vanilla into a large bowl. Whisk until really thick, pale, and creamy. Cool slightly. In a separate bowl, whisk the egg whites until stiff and almost forming peaks. In a third bowl, whip the cream until it is stiff and holds its shape. Stir the gelatin mixture, along with the Amaretto, into the beaten yolks. Then fold in the whipped cream, apricot purée, and lastly the egg whites. When lightly but thoroughly blended, spoon into the ramekins, smooth the tops, and freeze for 2 to 3 hours.

To make the sauce, heat all but a few of the black currants in a saucepan with the sugar; cook for 4 to 5 minutes. Pour through a sieve to remove all the seeds, if you wish, then add the whole black currants to the pan. Set aside. To serve, take the ramekins out of the freezer 10 minutes before eating, peel off the paper, and make a hole in the center of the top. Heat the sauce at the last minute and pour a little into the middle. Serve the rest separately.

Serves 4

orange sherbet

see variations page 149

Crisp and refreshingly light, but add more sugar to taste.

1 cup whole or low-fat milk	1 cup orange juice
2/3 cup superfine sugar	4 tbsp. marmalade
finely grated zest of 2 large oranges	juice and grated zest of 1 small orange

Mix together the milk, sugar, orange zest, and orange juice. Chill, stirring occasionally, until the sugar has dissolved. Transfer to an ice cream maker and process according to the manufacturer's directions, or pour into a freezer container and use the hand-mixing method (page 8). When almost firm, leave in the freezer for at least 15 minutes or until required.

To make the topping, heat the marmalade with the orange juice and zest, cool a little, then pour over the sherbet. Or just serve the sherbet simply with a twist of orange rind.

This sherbet can be stored in the freezer for up to 3 months. Take out 5 to 10 minutes before serving to soften.

Makes 1 pint

apple & plum parfait

see variations page 150

In France, a parfait is lighter and softer than a gelato or rich ice cream and especially good with tangy fruits. It is best just softly frozen. In the United States, a parfait is a frozen layered dessert. This parfait is both types.

3 large, ripe sweet plums
2 tbsp. demerara sugar
4 tbsp. water
2 sweet eating apples

1 cup granulated sugar
juice and finely grated zest of 1/2 lemon
5 egg yolks
1/2 cup plus 2 tbsp. heavy cream

Pit and roughly chop the plums, and put them in a small saucepan with the demerara sugar and water. Simmer gently until the plums are soft but not falling apart. Set aside half the plums to chill, then add the peeled, cored, and grated apples to the saucepan. Continue cooking until the fruit is soft enough to blend or mash. Cool completely. Slowly heat the granulated sugar with the lemon juice in another small pan until the sugar has dissolved. Boil for 2 to 3 minutes, then remove from the heat. Whisk the egg yolks in a large bowl until they have doubled in size. Then slowly whisk in the lemon sugar syrup and lemon zest, and continue whisking until thick and creamy. Cool completely.

When both the mashed fruit and the egg mixture are cool, whip the cream until it forms peaks. Carefully fold first the fruit mixture and then the whipped cream into the whisked egg yolks. Spoon into a small, deep freezer container and freeze until frozen around the sides. Beat with a fork until smooth, and then freeze until firm but not hard. To serve, put a spoonful of the reserved cooked plums into the base of chilled glasses, add a few scoops of parfait, and top with more plums. Serve immediately or chill briefly.

Serves 4

banana custard ice cream

see variations page 151

Turn this favorite taste combination very quickly into your family's favorite ice cream.

4 ripe bananas, plus more for serving
juice of 1 lemon
6 tbsp. clear honey
1 tsp. pure vanilla extract
1 cup homemade or store-bought vanilla
    custard

1 cup heavy cream, softly whipped, plus more
    for serving
caramel shards (page 14)

In a blender or food processor, blend the bananas with the lemon juice, honey, and vanilla until creamy smooth. Blend the mixture into the custard evenly and then fold in the whipped cream.

Spoon the mixture into a freezer container. Freeze for 1 hour, then break up with a fork until smooth again. Return to the freezer until firm or until ready to serve.

Serve scoops of the ice cream with more banana slices and whipped cream and a scattering of caramel shards.

This ice cream will freeze for up to 1 month. Remove from the freezer 15 minutes or more before serving to soften slightly.

Serves 6

tropical fruit sherbet

see variations page 152

A mixture of tropical fruits gives a wonderfully exotic taste, but you may use whatever is available at the time you shop. In fact, when you find some of these fruits in the store, this sherbet is a very good way to first try them.

2 cups peeled and chopped ripe tropical fruits
   (guava, pineapple, mango, papaya)
1 cup sugar syrup (page 11)

2 limes
1 cup whole milk or buttermilk

Purée or blend the tropical fruit, then press through a fine-mesh sieve if you like a really smooth texture.

Beat in the sugar syrup, finely grated rind of 1 lime and the juice of both, and the milk. Pour into a freezer container and freeze, using the hand-mixing method (page 8), breaking up two or three times during freezing.

Freeze until firm, then scoop into halved, small pineapple shells or serving dishes and sprinkle with freshly grated nutmeg. Serve with small tropical fruits such as lychee, or grapes, or toasted shreds of fresh coconut.

This ice cream can be frozen for up to 1 month. Remove from the freezer 10 minutes before serving to soften.

Makes about 1 1/2 pints

iced rhubarb delight

see variations page 153

This strange and seasonal fruit has a unique sweet taste and soft pink color that makes a stunning ice cream.

3 cups chopped, trimmed rhubarb
1/2 cup superfine sugar
1 to 2 tsp. pure vanilla extract

1/4 tsp. ground cinnamon
1 cup heavy cream, stiffly whipped
1 cup plain yogurt

Put the rhubarb, sugar, and vanilla into a small saucepan and simmer for about 8 minutes until very tender. Alternatively, cook in the microwave on medium for 3 or 4 minutes, stirring occasionally.

Purée the fruit, stir in the cinnamon, and set aside until cold.

Fold together the puréed rhubarb, the whipped cream, and the yogurt. Spoon into the bowl of an ice cream maker and process, following the manufacturer's instructions, or pour into a freezer container and freeze as directed on page 8. When the ice cream is firm, freeze briefly before serving, or until required.

This ice cream can be frozen for up to 3 months. Remove from the freezer 15 minutes before serving to soften slightly.

Makes about 2 1/4 pints

variations

summer berry semifreddo

see base recipe page 129

strawberry semifreddo with fraise & wild berries
Use only strawberries in the basic recipe and replace the brandy with fraise.
Serve with tiny wild berries, if possible.

gooseberry & muscat semifreddo
Prepare the basic recipe, using gooseberries cooked with 1/4 cup extra sugar,
and replace the brandy with Muscat wine.

black currant & cassis semifreddo
Prepare the basic semifreddo recipe, using all black currants (add extra sugar
to taste) and replace the brandy with cassis.

blueberry & chocolate liqueur semifreddo
When preparing the basic recipe, use only blueberries and replace the brandy
with chocolate liqueur. Serve topped with grated white chocolate.

currant semifreddo
Prepare the basic recipe, using red, white, or black currants (one only or a
mixture), and adding extra sugar to taste.

variations

iced blackberry & pear romanoff

see base recipe page 131

iced blackberry & apple romanoff
When preparing the basic recipe, replace the pear purée with apple purée.
Serve with a shot of Calvados.

iced blackberry & pineapple romanoff
Prepare the basic recipe, replacing the pear purée with crushed pineapple.
Omit the lemon zest.

iced cherry & apple romanoff
Prepare the basic recipe but replace the pear purée with apple purée and
the blackberries with pitted and chopped black cherries.

iced raspberry & pear romanoff
Replace the blackberries of the basic recipe with raspberries.

blackberry & black cherry romanoff
Prepare the basic recipe, replacing the pear purée with pitted ripe
black cherries.

variations

peach & passion fruit swirl ice cream

see base recipe page 132

peach & raspberry swirl ice cream
Prepare the basic recipe, replacing the passion fruit swirl with 1/4 cup raspberries puréed with 1 tablespoon superfine sugar.

peach & black currant swirl ice cream
Prepare the basic recipe, replacing the passion fruit swirl with 1/4 cup black (or red) currants cooked and puréed with 2 to 3 tablespoons superfine sugar (chill before adding to the ice cream).

nectarine & marmalade swirl ice cream
When preparing the basic recipe, use nectarines instead of peaches and replace the passion fruit swirl with 4 tablespoons fine-cut marmalade melted with 2 tablespoons orange juice, cooled.

nectarine & chocolate swirl ice cream
Prepare the basic ice cream recipe, using nectarines instead of peaches and replacing the passion fruit swirl with 1/4 cup white or dark chocolate sauce (page 13) cooled.

variations

iced apricot soufflés

see base recipe page 135

apricot & kirsch soufflés
Prepare the basic recipe but replace the Amaretto with kirsch and the black currants with black cherries.

peach soufflés
When preparing the basic recipe, replace the apricots with peaches or nectarines and the black currants with raspberries.

banana & praline soufflés
Prepare the basic recipe, replacing the apricots with bananas. When ready to serve, remove the paper and carefully dip the sides of the soufflés into crushed hazelnut praline (page 14). Serve with or without a sauce.

iced syllabub soufflés
Prepare the basic recipe, replacing the Amaretto and apricot purée with 1 1/4 cups good dessert wine. Serve with crisp cookies or tuiles (page 16).

variations

orange sherbet

see base recipe page 136

lemon sherbet
Prepare the basic recipe, replacing the orange zest and juice with fresh lemon zest and juice. This is very sharp and perfect as a refresher between courses at a special dinner, or add more sugar to taste and serve with a little Cointreau poured on top.

pineapple sherbet
When preparing the basic recipe, replace 1/2 cup of the orange juice with up to 3/4 cup very ripe peeled and grated pineapple. Serve with fresh pineapple wedges and mint leaves.

passion fruit sherbet
Prepare the basic recipe but replace 1/2 cup of the orange juice with the pulp of 4 passion fruit with seeds.

ruby grapefruit sherbet
Replace the orange juice and zest of basic recipe with the same amount of ruby grapefruit juice and zest. Freeze and serve in grapefruit shells.

variations

apple & plum parfait

see base recipe page 139

green apple & greengage parfait
Prepare the basic recipe, using unpeeled green-skinned apples and
greengage plums.

apple & mixed berries parfait
Replace the plums of the basic recipe with mixed berries.

pear & plum parfait
Prepare the basic parfait recipe, but replace the apples with ripe pears. Serve
the parfaits sprinkled with toasted nuts.

apple & calvados parfait
Prepare the basic recipe, omitting the plums. Cook 3 grated apples with the
sugar and water. Mix half the apples with 4 tablespoons Calvados, then chill.
Continue as described, serving a little cooked apple and Calvados in the base
of the glasses and a little on the top instead of plums. Serve with a glass of
iced Calvados.

variations

banana custard ice cream

see base recipe page 140

banana & coconut custard ice cream
Prepare the basic recipe, stirring in 1/4 cup shredded coconut before freezing. Serve sprinkled with toasted coconut instead of the original toppings.

banana & nougat custard ice cream
When preparing the basic recipe, stir in 1/3 cup chopped nougat just before freezing. Serve sprinkled with toasted sliced almonds and confectioners' sugar instead of the original toppings.

banana custard & jelly ripple ice cream
Prepare the basic ice cream and when it is ready for the final freezing, swirl in 6 tablespoons raspberry or black cherry jelly.

banana & taffy custard ice cream
Just before freezing the basic recipe stir in 1/3 cup chopped apple sour taffy or another chewy apple candy.

banana custard ice cream with peanut butter ripple
Prepare the basic recipe and just before freezing stir in 1/2 cup smooth peanut butter.

variations

tropical fruit sherbet

see base recipe page 143

tropical sherbet with rum
Prepare the basic recipe, replacing half the milk with white rum. Serve with a little pink grenadine poured over the top and lots of fresh fruit.

tropical sherbet with pineapple sauce
Serve the basic recipe topped with pineapple sauce (page 14).

coconut cream tropics
Prepare the basic recipe replacing the milk with coconut milk or cream. Serve topped with flakes of fresh coconut, toasted.

piña colada sherbet
Prepare the basic recipe, using only pineapple. Replace the sugar syrup with light rum and the milk with coconut milk. Serve in coconut shells.

tropical banana sherbet
When preparing the basic recipe, replace the sugar syrup with crème de banane (banana liqueur).

variations

iced rhubarb delight

see base recipe page 144

iced rhubarb & ginger classic
Prepare the basic recipe, replacing the cinnamon with 1 teaspoon ground ginger
and 2 whole stem gingers, finely grated. Serve in ginger snap baskets (page 17).

iced rhubarb & orange delight
Orange has an uncanny way of bringing out the best in rhubarb. Prepare the basic
recipe, adding the finely grated zest and juice of 1 large orange to the cooked
rhubarb. Serve the ice cream with slices or wedges of caramelized oranges.

iced rhubarb & raspberry delight
This makes an ice cream with a fabulous color and a great taste. Prepare the basic
recipe, replacing 1 cup of rhubarb with 1 cup of raspberries, but don't cook them.
Purée the raspberries straight into the bowl of cooked rhubarb and continue as
directed.

iced rhubarb & oat crumble
Process 2 tablespoons unsalted butter, 1/4 cup all-purpose flour, 1/8 cup rolled oats,
and 1 tablespoon demerara sugar in a processor briefly. Spread onto foil on a
baking pan and bake at 400°F (200°C) until crisp and turning golden. Cool and then
crumble. Prepare the basic recipe, but before the final freezing, stir in the cooled
crumble mix.

iced treats for kids

Ice cream is nearly always at the top of the treats
list for the young in the family, but for parties and
special occasions, it is nice to make an extra effort.
These fun ideas will have your young guests lining
up and begging for first choice. You may even be
able to get them to help you for a change!

frozen chocolate bananas

see variations page 170

Frozen bananas offer the perfect contrast between crunchy chocolate and soft, melting banana.

4 firm but ripe small bananas
6 oz. milk chocolate, broken into chunks
6 tbsp. heavy cream
4 tbsp. orange juice

Freeze the bananas in their skins for about 2 hours.

Melt the chocolate in a small pan with the cream and orange juice, stirring occasionally until melted and smooth. Pour into a cold bowl and leave until it just begins to thicken and cool. Don't let it get too cold otherwise it will not coat easily.

Take the bananas out of the freezer and remove their skins neatly. Dip each banana into the chocolate to coat thoroughly, then remove it using one or two long wooden skewers. Hold the banana over the bowl while the excess chocolate drips off. Then place the banana on waxed paper until the chocolate sets. Cut into 2 or 3 pieces and return to the freezer until ready to serve. Insert a popsicle stick into each piece for serving, if you wish.

These bananas do not keep well and should be eaten on the day they are made.

Serves 4

ice cream cookie sandwich

see variations page 171

The ultimate sandwich—your favorite cookies sandwiched with your favorite ice cream. Vary the flavor combination as you wish and use cookie cutters to make different shapes.

12 chocolate cookies
2 cups vanilla (or other flavor) ice cream, softened

Place the cookies on a tray in the freezer.

Spread the softened ice cream in a flat pan or container to about 1/2-inch thickness and refreeze. When firm again, but not hard, cut 6 circles of ice cream to fit the cookies. Carefully transfer the ice cream from the pan onto 6 cookies.

Top with a second cookie. Press down to seal well and freeze until ready to eat. If well frozen, remove from the freezer 10 to 15 minutes before you want to eat them otherwise they will be very hard.

Eat within a couple of days.

Serves 6

icy fruit dippers

see variations page 172

Almost the reverse of a fondue, this will make a great end to a summer family barbecue. Be sure you have a good choice of sweet dips ready.

3 to 4 cups (1 1/2 to 2 lbs.) good-quality firm
   fresh fruits (strawberries, cherries,
   cape gooseberries)
1 cup heavy cream, sweetened and whipped

3/4 cup raspberry sauce (page 14)
3/4 cup mango sauce (page 14)
candy sprinkles

Prepare the fruit simply by wiping or checking them over, but leave on their stems or anything they can be picked up by. Freeze them separately on waxed paper on baking sheets for at least 1 hour until icy but not too hard.

Set out bowls of whipped cream, raspberry and mango sauces, and sprinkles. Arrange the frosted fruits, with toothpicks, on a large serving platter and serve.

Serves 6

sticky toffee treats

see variations page 173

Toffee and vanilla ice cream is always going to be a winner. Serve this in cones for the perfect summer dessert.

1 cup toffee sauce (page 13)
3 cups vanilla ice cream
4 sugar cones

If you have a line of impatient youngsters, you will need to be well-prepared. Bring the sauce to room temperature so it is thick but easy to pour. Have the ice cream ready to scoop. Have cones ready in a holder.

Take 2 or 3 spoonfuls of sauce and spread it over the top of the ice cream. Then quickly take out a scoop of ice cream, swirling the sauce through at the same time, and put it in the cone. Repeat if you want a second scoop on the same cone.

Add a final drizzle of sauce over the top. Serve immediately.

Serves 4

fruity ice cubes

see variations page 174

Healthy frozen yogurt cubes make a quick and really easy dessert for a very young audience. In fact, youngsters can help you make them, which will add to the fun.

1 cup puréed raspberries
1 cup plain or fruit yogurt

Mix the fruit and yogurt together. Pour into large, easy-release ice cube trays or fruit-shaped ice trays. Smooth the tops so they are completely flat to help them come out easily. Insert small popsicle sticks, if you wish.

Freeze for 3 to 4 hours or overnight. Turn out onto a pretty platter and serve with pieces of fresh fruit and cookies.

Makes 10 to 12 large cubes

iced fruit pops

see variations page 175

Freshly crushed fruit and juice frozen in popsicle containers make refreshing summer ice pops—and you know they are not full of sugar and colorings!

1 1/2 cups grated or puréed fresh fruit (pineapple, peach, mango)
sugar to taste
1/2 cup (4 fl oz) orange juice concentrate

Mix the puréed fruit with the sugar and orange juice. Freeze in popsicle containers until partly frozen. Stir once to mix the fruit around, then refreeze until almost set.

Place a popsicle stick in the center of each pop and freeze until hard.

Eat straight from the freezer. Preferably eat as soon as possible or freeze for no more than 1 month in covered containers.

Makes 4 to 6 (depending on size of molds)

ice cream cupcakes

see variations page 176

These cute ice cream cupcakes can be topped with whipped cream, fruit, or sprinkles. Little girls will love them. Serve them in multicolored paper baking cups or remove the paper before serving.

2 cups strawberry ice cream (page 38)
6 tbsp. heavy cream, whipped

12 fresh raspberries
candy sprinkles

Place 6 paper or foil baking cups in a muffin pan. If using very thin paper baking cups, double them for extra support.

When the ice cream is at a soft, spoonable consistency, fill the baking cups and flatten the tops. Return to the freezer until almost ready to serve.

To serve, remove the baking cups if you wish and place the ice cakes on a well-chilled serving plate. Top each ice with a little whipped cream, 2 raspberries, and a shake of sprinkles. Return to the freezer until ready to eat.

These little ice cakes are not really for keeping longer than a day, so try to make only as many as you need.

Serves 6

crunchy yogurt shapes

see variations page 177

Greek yogurt and honey make the simplest, most delicious, and healthy ice cream. Make it into animal shapes for a bit of fun, then coat with sprinkles.

1 cup good thick honey
3 cups thick Greek yogurt
1 cup heavy cream, lightly whipped

1 tsp. pure vanilla extract
candy sprinkles

Warm the honey very slightly just to soften it. Stir in the yogurt, whipped cream, and vanilla, and pour into a shallow container to freeze, stirring with a fork once or twice. Freeze for 1 hour, break up with a fork, and freeze for another hour until firm but spoonable.

Line a sheet pan with nonstick paper. Place animal-shaped or other cookie cutters on the pan and fill with the ice cream, making sure to level the tops. Quickly return to the freezer for 1 to 2 hours until really firm.

When ready to serve, carefully push the ice cream out of the molds onto an ice-cold plate. Allow 1 or 2 minutes for the surface to begin to soften. Then, using one or two wooden skewers, dip them on one or two sides into a bowl of sprinkles. Return to the freezer immediately, because they will start to melt very quickly.

To serve, insert a popsicle stick into each one.

Makes about 6 to 10 shapes depending on molds

variations

frozen chocolate bananas

see base recipe page 155

white chocolate banana pops
Prepare the basic recipe, but use white chocolate instead of milk chocolate.

double chocolate banana pops
When preparing the basic recipe, dip the bananas into the chocolate, then into chocolate sprinkles or chocolate chips.

nutty banana pops
Prepare the basic recipe. After dipping in chocolate, coat immediately in praline mixture (page 14) or, for a less rich version, in very finely chopped toasted nuts.

crunchy banana pops
Prepare the basic recipe. After dipping in chocolate, coat immediately in crushed cornflakes, crispy rice cereal, or toasted breadcrumbs.

banana—mallow pops
Instead of chocolate-covered pops, make marshmallow ones. Cut the peeled frozen bananas into 4 or 5 pieces. Put each piece on a small wooden skewer. Melt 6 ounces of marshmallows slowly (in the microwave is best). When everyone is ready, hand around the banana sticks to dip immediately into the soft marshmallow. This is messy. These are not for keeping!

variations

ice cream cookie sandwich

see base recipe page 156

mocha ice cream sandwich
Use circles of freshly cooked chocolate cake instead of cookies, and coffee ice cream instead of vanilla.

old-fashioned ice cream sandwich
Coat old-fashioned sugar wafer cookies with a layer of chocolate. Freeze, then sandwich with butter pecan or peanut butter ice cream.

fruit & nut ice cream sandwich
Prepare the basic recipe, using oatmeal cookies instead of chocolate. Spread them with strawberry jam and sandwich them with raspberry ripple gelato (page 58).

lemon shortbread ice cream sandwich
Prepare the basic recipe, using lemon shortbread cookies spread with marmalade or lemon curd. Use lemon gelato (page 61) or vanilla ice cream (page 19).

variations

icy fruit dippers

see base recipe page 159

icy kabobs
Prepare the basic recipe, replacing the fruits with wedges of apples, pears, and pineapple. Dip them in lemon juice, arrange 3 to 4 pieces on small bamboo sticks or skewers, and freeze as directed. Serve with whipped cream, sauces, and sprinkles.

yogurt dippers
Prepare a selection of frosted soft fruits on small sticks (or tiny forks if this is for little children) in bowls. Serve with a selection of yogurts to dip into.

icy fruit dippers with chocolate dip
Follow the basic recipe, but replace the fruit sauces with hot chocolate sauce (page 13). Watch how the sauce starts to set when you dip your fruit!

icy fruit dippers with caramel dip
Prepare the basic recipe, but replace the fruit sauces with hot butterscotch sauce (page 13). Serve the fruits on longer sticks if the sauce is very hot.

sticky toffee treats

see base recipe page 160

caramel stick cones
Prepare the basic recipe, adding a few long thin shards of caramel (page 14) to each cone.

banana cones
Cut 1 banana into thin sticks about 2 inches long. Dip each stick in lemon juice. Freeze for 1 hour. Add 1 or 2 to each toffee cone when serving.

apple cones
Core and cut an apple into thin wedges and dip in lemon juice. Freeze for 1 hour. Add 1 or 2 wedges to each toffee cone when serving.

chocolate toffee cases
Instead of cones, serve the ice cream with toffee sauce in chocolate cups (page 15).

toffee waffles
Instead of cones, use warmed or toasted waffles. Add frozen fruits too, if you wish.

variations

fruity ice cubes

see base recipe page 163

mango ice cubes
Follow the basic recipe, replacing the raspberries with puréed mango.
Serve with fresh raspberry sauce (page 14).

chocolate yogurt cubes
Prepare the basic recipe, omitting the berries, doubling the yogurt, and
adding 3 tablespoons sifted chocolate milk powder.

saucy fruity ice cubes
Serve the basic recipe with hot chocolate sauce (page 13) to dip into.

toffee-dipped fruity ice cubes
Prepare the basic recipe and serve with hot toffee sauce (page 13) to
dip into.

pineapple cubes
Replace the raspberries of the basic recipe with crushed pineapple. Serve
with raspberry sauce (page 14).

iced fruit pops

see base recipe page 164

iced raspberry crush pops
Prepare the basic recipe, replacing the fruit with crushed raspberries and the orange juice with raspberry juice, cranberry juice, or raspberry cordial (for an adult version).

iced black & blueberry pops
When preparing the basic recipe, replace the fruit with crushed and strained ripe blackberries and black currants and the orange juice with blueberry juice (or cassis for an adult version).

iced bananas & cream pops
Prepare the basic recipe, using 1 1/2 cups mashed or puréed bananas, 1/2 cup heavy cream, and 2 tablespoons orange or lemon juice.

iced strawberry milk pops
Follow the basic recipe, using crushed strawberries (strained if you wish) and milk instead of juice. Add sugar and vanilla to taste.

variations

ice cream cupcakes

see base recipe page 167

vanilla ice cakes with raspberry sauce
Prepare the basic recipe, omitting the raspberries and sprinkles. Serve the
cakes topped with hulled fresh strawberries and raspberry sauce (page 14).

raspberry ripple ice cakes
Follow the basic recipe, substituting raspberry ripple gelato (page 58) for the
strawberry ice cream. Top with a pile of various berries and sprinkle with
sifted confectioners' sugar. Drizzle with raspberry sauce.

chocolate whip ice cakes
Prepare the basic recipe, substituting white chocolate swirl gelato (page 70).
Top with piped whipped cream and drizzle with chocolate sauce (page 13).
Finish with grated chocolate or chocolate sprinkles.

cheesecake ice cakes
Prepare the basic recipe, using New York cheesecake ice cream (page 23). Top
with a layer of the graham cracker mix before freezing. Add a few pieces of
chopped fresh apricot and a swirl of whipped cream or thick Greek yogurt.

peanut butter ice cakes with mango & mallow
Follow the basic recipe, using crunchy peanut butter ice cream (page 28),
topped with pieces of mango and chopped marshmallows.

variations

crunchy yogurt shapes

see base recipe page 168

crispie yogurt shapes
Prepare the yogurt ices as directed, but coat in lightly crushed chocolate crispy rice cereal instead of the candy sprinkles.

crunchy nutty yogurt shapes
Prepare basic recipe but coat in lightly crushed, crunchy nutty cereal instead of the candy sprinkles.

chocolate yogurt shapes
Coat the yogurt ices in a crumbled chocolate candy bar or grated chocolate instead of the candy sprinkles.

berry fruity yogurt shapes
Prepare the yogurt ices. While freezing, finely chop 1/2 cup dried blueberries, cranberries, cherries, or your favorite dried fruits. Coat the yogurt ices with these instead of the candy sprinkles.

candy fruit yogurt shapes
Prepare the yogurt ices as directed, but coat them with candies, such as M&Ms.

sundaes, sodas & slushes

Get out those frivolous sundae dishes and long tall glasses; whip up your favorite ice cream and luscious sauces; stock up on fruits, sodas, and sprinkles; and settle down to savor one of these tantalizing sundaes, floats, slushes, frappés, and smoothies.

knickerbocker glory

see variations page 198

Whether you like to believe this famous sundae is named for the early days of New York City, for the American Knickerbocker hotels, or the multicolored and striped long breeches worn in England in the 1900s, the knickerbocker glory is still a popular and flamboyant ice cream sundae.

fresh strawberries and cherries
2 scoops vanilla ice cream
6 to 8 tbsp. fruit jelly
strawberry or raspberry sauce (page 14)

2 scoops strawberry ice cream
1/2 cup heavy cream, whipped
toasted sliced almonds

Arrange a little fresh fruit in the base of two chilled sundae glasses. Add a scoop of vanilla ice cream, then some fruit jelly and some fruit sauce.

Next add strawberry ice cream, and then more fruit sauce. Now top with whipped cream, fresh fruit, and nuts, followed by more sauce and a few nuts. Return to the freezer for no more than 30 minutes or eat immediately.

These are not for keeping, so prepare as required. It is a good idea to have a selection of suitable ingredients ready before you start, as well as well-chilled glasses.

Serves 2

peach melba

see variations page 199

This classic sundae was created in the 1890s by the renowned chef, Escoffier, for the Australian soprano, Dame Nellie Melba. It contains some of the most delicious fresh fruits and flavors of summer.

4 large ripe peaches, peeled
finely grated zest and juice of 1 lemon
2 to 3 tbsp. confectioners' sugar
8 scoops vanilla ice cream

for the melba sauce
1 1/2 cups ripe raspberries
2 tbsp. red currant jelly
2 tbsp. superfine sugar

Cut the peaches in half and remove the pits. Tightly pack the peach halves in an ovenproof dish and brush with lemon juice. Sprinkle generously with confectioners' sugar. Put the dish under a preheated broiler for 5 to 7 minutes or until golden and bubbling. Let cool.

To make the sauce, warm the raspberries with the jelly and sugar, and then press them through a sieve. Let cool.

Arrange the peaches on a serving platter with 1 or 2 scoops of ice cream. Drizzle with melba sauce and finish with shreds of lemon zest.

Serves 4

cappuccino frappé

see variations page 200

Icy cold but not quite frozen, this alcoholic coffee ice is delicious as a midafternoon treat or after dinner.

4 tbsp. coffee liqueur
1/2 recipe coffee gelato (page 63)
4 tbsp. rum

1/2 cup heavy cream, whipped
1 tbsp. unsweetened cocoa powder, sifted

Pour the liqueur into the base of 6 freezer-proof glasses or cups, and chill well or freeze.

Prepare the gelato as directed until partly frozen. Then whisk in the rum with an electric mixer until frothy, spoon immediately over the frozen liqueur, and freeze again until firm but not hard.

Pipe the whipped the cream over the gelato. Sprinkle generously with cocoa powder and return to the freezer for a few minutes until you are absolutely ready to serve.

Serves 6

iced lassi

see variations page 201

Lassi, an Indian yogurt-based drink, is served as a refresher in hot countries (where it's especially delightful after hot curries). It's also a great semi-iced drink for all types of hot occasions.

2 cups plain yogurt, partially frozen
1/2 cup ice water
1/2 cup ice cubes

4 tbsp. clear honey, plus more to taste
freshly grated nutmeg

Put the yogurt, ice water, ice cubes, and honey in a food processor or blender. Blend until frothy and well mixed. Transfer to iced tall glasses and freeze for about 30 minutes.

Serve with a little more honey to taste and sprinkle with freshly grated nutmeg.

Serves 1

ice cream float

see variations page 202

Ice cream floats, also known as ice cream sodas, can be as colorful and varied as you wish.

2 cups lemon–lime soda, chilled
2 scoops vanilla ice cream
a few mini-marshmallows

Put 1 scoop of ice cream into a chilled, tall soda glass. Pour the soda in slowly, because it will bubble up on contact with the ice cream.

Add the second scoop of ice cream and top with a few small marshmallows.

Serve immediately with a long soda spoon and straws.

Makes 1

watermelon & strawberry slush

see variations page 203

For a quick and refreshing summer ice or drink, a slush is great — fresh and fruity for the kids, alcoholic for the adults. If you want to serve it like an ice cone, pile up some crushed ice in a glass and pour the blended ingredients over the ice.

1 cup crushed ice
1 cup hulled and halved fresh strawberries
1 cup watermelon flesh (seeds removed)

2 to 3 tbsp. strawberry syrup or Fraise liqueur
slices of fresh fruit, to garnish

Place all the ingredients (reserve a few pieces of fruit for serving) in a blender or food processor. Blend briefly just to crush all the ingredients to a slush. Don't overblend. Place in a container in the freezer until ready to serve.

When required, scoop into tall glasses (or martini glasses) and serve topped with a few pieces of fruit.

Serves 1

188   sundaes, sodas & slushes

iced apricot & pomegranate smoothie

see variations page 204

Creamy smooth yogurt drinks are healthy and refreshing, especially when well iced. All the family will love them at any time of day.

1 cup plain or peach yogurt
2 cups chopped and pitted ripe apricots
2 to 3 tbsp. clear honey

a few ice cubes
1/2 pomegranate, broken up into seeds and
    white pith removed

Push the pomegranates through a sieve. Place the yogurt, apricots, honey, ice cubes, and pomegranate juice (reserve a spoonful of seeds) in a blender or food processor. Blend until really smooth.

Freeze briefly (up to 30 minutes) or enjoy immediately, topped with a spoonful of pomegranate seeds.

Serves 2

banana split

see variations page 205

This old-time favorite, often said to have been created in Wilmington, Ohio, has not lost its popularity with younger generations, who love as many ice cream flavors as possible all together.

1 firm ripe banana
1 scoop each chocolate, vanilla, and strawberry
    ice cream (see chapter 1)
1 tbsp. chocolate sauce (page 13)
1 tbsp. strawberry sauce (page 14)

cream, heavy or whipping
chopped nuts
maraschino cherries or strawberries
rolled wafers (optional)

Slice the banana in half lengthwise and place in an oval dessert dish. Top with a scoop of each flavor of ice cream.

Drizzle with a little of the two sauces, then top with the whipped cream, nuts, and fresh fruit. Add a rolled wafer as well, if you wish.

Serves 1

chocolate nut sundae

see variations page 206

Chocolate and nuts make so many wonderful combinations that it is hard to choose a favorite!

1 scoop rich chocolate ice cream (page 20)
1 scoop butter pecan ice cream (page 35)
2 tbsp. chocolate sauce (page 13)
2 tbsp. toasted mixed nuts
chocolate flakes, curls, or sprinkles

Arrange the two scoops of ice cream in a chilled sundae dish. Drizzle with chocolate sauce and then sprinkle with nuts and chocolate.

Serves 1

chocolate-dipped gelato pops

see variations page 207

Who can deny that a really good chocolate ice beats the lot on some occasions, especially when made with your own favorite ice cream?

1 recipe luxury vanilla gelato (page 53)
1 recipe chocolate sauce (page 13)
finely chopped nuts or sprinkles

Make the ice cream into scoops of various sizes. Place them immediately on waxed paper and refreeze really thoroughly.

Prepare the chocolate sauce and then leave in a cool (not cold) place until cooled but not thickening.

Cover several sheet pans with waxed paper. Push a popsicle stick into the center of a scoop of ice cream and dip it into the chocolate to completely cover. Hold it over the bowl of chocolate until it has finished dripping and then place it on the clean waxed paper.

Sprinkle with nuts or colored sprinkles if you wish. Put the ices in the freezer and leave until really hard (several hours). Although they will keep for several weeks, depending on the variety of ice cream used, it is better to eat them as soon as possible.

Makes 6–8 (more if using a very small scoop)

variations

knickerbocker glory

see base recipe page 179

cherryberry glory
Instead of the basic recipe, layer fresh blueberries with raspberry ripple gelato (page 58), black cherry jam, vanilla ice cream, and strawberry-flavored whipped cream (stir 2 tablespoons strawberry sauce into the whipped cream). Finish with maraschino cherries, ladyfingers, and strawberry sauce.

chocoholics' knickerbocker glory
Instead of the basic recipe, layer dark and white chocolate ice cream (page 20) with crumbled chocolate brownies, pitted black cherries, raspberry sauce, and whipped cream. Top with raspberries, chocolate curls or sprinkles, and hot chocolate fudge sauce (page 13).

morning glory
Layer fresh fruit with orange sherbet (page 136), thick and fruity yogurt, banana custard ice cream (page 140), whipped cream, and fresh passion fruit pulp. Sprinkle with toasted granola or oats and nuts.

bananabocker glory
Instead of the basic recipe, layer chocolate, banana custard, and crunchy peanut butter ice creams (pages 20, 140, and 28) with fudge and toffee sauces (page 13), slices of banana, marshmallows, peach sauce (page 14), and whipped cream. Finish with chocolate sprinkles and more marshmallows.

variations

peach melba

see base recipe page 180

pear melba
Prepare the basic recipe, replacing the peaches with broilled or poached pears.

pears belle hélène
Prepare the basic recipe but replace the peaches with pears and the melba sauce with chocolate sauce (page 13).

pineapple melba
When preparing the basic recipe, replace the peaches with slices of pineapple.

mango melba
Prepare the basic recipe, replacing the peaches with thick slices of peeled mango.

peach belle hélène
Prepare the basic recipe, replacing the melba sauce with hot chocolate sauce (page 13).

variations

cappuccino frappé

see base recipe page 183

espresso frappé
Prepare the basic recipe, replacing the coffee gelato with coffee granita (page 103) and the rum with cold espresso coffee.

mocha frappé
Prepare the basic recipe, replacing the coffee liqueur with chocolate liqueur.

vanilla frappé
Prepare the basic recipe, replacing the coffee gelato with luxury vanilla gelato (page 53).

almond frappé
When making the basic recipe, try replacing the rum with Amaretto and the cocoa powder with toasted flaked almonds.

orange frappé
Prepare the basic recipe, replacing the rum with orange liqueur and the cocoa powder with a little grated zest of orange.

variations

iced lassi

see base recipe page 184

iced spiced lassi
Quickly fry 1 teaspoon cumin seeds in a small dry pan, stirring frequently, until they smell wonderful but not burnt. Grind the seeds or pound them in a mortar. Prepare the basic recipe, omitting the honey and nutmeg, Add the ground cumin, 1/4 teaspoon red chile flakes, and a pinch salt before freezing.

iced mango lassi
Prepare the basic recipe, adding the flesh of 1/2 ripe mango to the blender before processing.

iced papaya lassi
Prepare the basic recipe, adding the pulp of 1/2 ripe papaya to the blender before processing.

iced refresher lassi
When preparing the basic recipe, add the finely grated zest and the juice of 1 lemon to the blender before processing.

variations

ice cream float

see base recipe page 187

red raspberry float
Instead of the basic recipe, use strawberry or raspberry soda and raspberry water ice (page 112). Top with fresh raspberries and a few nuts.

chocolate cream float
Prepare the basic recipe, using chocolate ice cream instead of vanilla. Top with whipped cream and a drizzle of chocolate sauce.

brown cow float
Prepare the basic recipe, using cola and whipped cream instead of marshmallows.

double brown cow float
Instead of the basic recipe, use a cola beverage and chocolate ice cream. Top with grated chocolate.

root beer (black) float
Prepare the basic recipe, using root beer instead of lemon-lime soda, and finish with a drizzle of chocolate sauce.

boston cooler
For this recipe, use ginger ale instead of lemon-lime soda and sprinkles instead of marshmallows.

variations

watermelon & strawberry slush

see base recipe page 188

watermelon & raspberry slush
Prepare the basic recipe, replacing the strawberries with raspberries and the syrup with lime juice.

piña colada slush
Prepare the basic recipe, replacing the strawberries with crushed pineapple and the watermelon with well-chilled coconut cream. Replace the strawberry syrup or fraise with a topping of white rum at the last minute.

bloody mary slush
Replace all the strawberries and melon in the basic recipe with 2 cups of tomato juice. Add a generous dash of Worcestershire sauce, lemon juice, salt, and pepper. Blend with the ice as directed in recipe and place in freezer. When ready to serve, add a shot of vodka.

melon martini slush
Prepare the basic recipe, replacing the strawberries with cantaloupe and omitting the syrup. When ready to serve, scoop into martini glasses with a shot of martini and a wedge of melon.

iced apricot & pomegranate smoothie

see base recipe page 191

iced blueberry passion smoothie
Prepare the basic recipe, replacing the apricots with blueberries and the pomegranate with the pulp of 1 passion fruit.

iced avocado cream smoothie
Prepare the basic recipe, using vanilla yogurt, replacing the apricots with avocado, and the pomegranate with the finely grated zest and juice of 1/2 lime.

iced pink grapefruit smoothie
Replace the apricots of the basic recipe with 2 pink grapefruits. Add extra honey to taste and finish with the pomegranate.

iced pink berry smoothie
Prepare the basic recipe, replacing the apricots with ripe seasonal berries or currants. Add extra honey, depending on the fruit, and top with a couple of berries or currants.

iced sharon fruit smoothie
When preparing the basic recipe, replace the apricots with the flesh of 2 ripe Sharon fruit (persimmons).

variations

banana split

see base recipe page 192

banana & raspberry split
Instead of the basic recipe, use banana custard ice cream (page 140), vanilla
ice cream (page 19), and raspberry ripple gelato (page 58). Top with
chocolate and raspberry sauces (pages 13 and 14), sprinkles, and fresh
raspberries.

banana toffee split
Instead of the basic recipe, use banana custard, vanilla, and butter pecan
ice creams (pages 140, 19, and 35). Top with toffee and chocolate sauces
(page 13), strawberries, chopped nuts, and whipped cream.

tropical banana split
Instead of the basic recipe, use tropical fruit sherbet (page 143), mango
sorbet (page 82), and vanilla ice cream (page 19). Top with pineapple and
fudge sauces (page 13 and 14), fresh pineapple, chopped nuts, chocolate
sprinkles, and whipped cream.

chocolate banana split
Instead of the basic recipe, use chocolate and vanilla ice creams with
chocolate sauce and toffee sauce (page 13), then sprinkle with nuts,
chocolate sprinkles, and whipped cream.

variations

chocolate nut sundae

see base recipe page 195

mint chocolate sundae
Instead of the basic recipe, use a scoop each of butter pecan ice cream and
Bailey's mint chocolate gelato (page 70). Drizzle with a mint liqueur, sprinkle
on crushed or crumbled mint candies, and finish with chocolate sauce
(page 13) and toasted nuts.

orange chocolate sundae
Try using a scoop each of bitter chocolate gelato (page 57) and butter pecan
ice cream. Sprinkle with shreds of orange rind, orange liqueur, chocolate
sauce, orange and chocolate sprinkles, whipped cream, and toasted pecans.

chocolate pistachio sundae
Instead of the basic recipe, use a scoop each of bitter chocolate gelato
(page 57) and pistachio gelato (page 54). Top with chocolate sauce
(page 13), grated chocolate or chocolate sprinkles, whipped cream, chopped
walnuts, and pistachios.

mocha sundae
Instead of the basic recipe, use a scoop each of rocky road ice cream
(page 32) and coffee gelato (page 63). Top with fudge sauce (page 13),
coffee syrup (page 12), whipped cream, grated chocolate, and toasted nuts.

variations

chocolate-dipped gelato pops

see base recipe page 196

strawberry gelato pops with white chocolate coating
Follow the basic recipe, using strawberry gelato (page 50). Make the chocolate sauce with white chocolate.

coffee gelato pops with milk chocolate coating
Prepare the basic recipe using coffee gelato (page 63). Make the chocolate sauce with milk chocolate.

pistachio gelato pops with dark chocolate coating
Follow the basic recipe, using pistachio gelato (page 54). Coat with dark chocolate sauce.

after-dinner gelato pops
For an occasional after-dinner treat, use a small melon baller to make very small scoops or balls of blood orange sorbet (page 95) or another favorite ice cream. Dip the balls into the prepared chocolate sauce as described (and into sprinkles too, if you wish) and then transfer straight to the freezer. Serve on a plate over ice so they stay frozen for as long as possible.

ice cream gateaux, bombes & terrines

These are the showstoppers of the ice cream world! All these glamorous desserts can be made in advance when you have plenty of time and, with only a few last-minute touches, will make entertaining easy.

frozen macaroon terrine

see variations page 225

This Italian favorite is sublimely sweet and nutty, especially when coated with praline, and it's so easy to make. The perfect party dessert.

2 egg whites
1/2 cup confectioners' sugar, sifted
2 cups heavy cream, softly whipped
1 cup crushed macaroons

3 tbsp. Amaretto liqueur
1 cup crushed almond praline (page 15)
chocolate curls or shapes, to decorate

Whisk the egg whites until stiff, and then fold in the sugar until thick and glossy.

In another bowl, whip the cream until stiff, then fold in the crushed macaroons and Amaretto. Fold into the egg whites.

Spoon into a 3 x 11-inch terrine pan or loaf pan and freeze overnight until completely firm.

When ready to serve, turn it out onto a folded sheet of foil. Have the praline on another sheet. Carefully coat the terrine with the crushed praline, pressing gently with a palette knife to coat all but the base. Transfer the terrine to a serving platter and decorate with the pieces of chocolate.

Serves 8–10

chocolate & cherry ice cream gateau

see variations page 226

Layers of chocolate cake, vanilla ice cream, and sweet black cherry filling make a delicious and stunning centerpiece.

1 cup (2 sticks) unsalted butter
1 cup superfine sugar
1 tsp. pure vanilla extract
4 eggs, beaten
2 cups less 1 heaped tbsp. all-purpose flour
1 heaped tbsp. unsweetened cocoa powder
1 1/2 tsp. baking powder

4 cups pitted and chopped cherries
1/2 cup cranberry juice
3 tbsp. light brown sugar
1/2 recipe luxury vanilla gelato (page 53)
1 cup heavy cream, softly whipped
few cherries for topping
chocolate curls

Preheat the oven to 350°F (180°C). Lightly grease a 7-inch springform or loose-bottomed deep cake pan. Beat the butter, sugar, and vanilla together until pale and creamy. Gently beat in half the eggs, then gradually fold in the dry ingredients, alternating with the rest of the eggs, until well blended. Spoon into the prepared cake pan, flatten the top, and bake for 35 to 40 minutes until just firm to the touch. Cool in the pan, then remove, wrap in foil, and refrigerate until really cold, to make slicing easier.

Put the cherries in a small saucepan with the cranberry juice and brown sugar. Cook over moderate heat until tender. Set aside to cool, then refrigerate until really cold. Prepare the vanilla gelato until it reaches a spoonable consistency.

With a long knife, cut the cake into three even layers. Place one layer into the 7-inch cake pan, and top with half the cherries and one-third of their juice. Cover with a layer of gelato, and then the second cake layer. Add the rest of the cherries but not all the juice (use the rest of the juice to moisten the underside of the third cake layer). Cover with the rest of the gelato and the final cake layer. Press down well, cover with plastic wrap, and freeze overnight. (If desired, the cake can be stored in the freezer for up to 1 month.)

To serve, carefully remove the cake pan and slide the gateau out onto a chilled serving plate. Top with the whipped cream, chocolate curls, and fresh cherries. Return to the freezer until ready to serve.

Serves 8–10

chocolate bombe

see variations page 227

Ice cream bombes look exotic but can be surprisingly simple. Just use a good ice cream for the outer layer, surrounding a light, sweet, mousse filling.

1/2 recipe bitter chocolate gelato (page 57)
1/2 cup whipping cream
1 small egg white

1/8 cup superfine sugar
4 oz. fresh raspberries, mashed and strained
1 recipe raspberry sauce (page 14)

In the freezer, chill a 3 1/2 to 4-cup bombe mold or metal bowl. Prepare the gelato. When it is a spreadable consistency, set the mold into a bowl of ice. Line the inside of the mold with gelato, making sure it is a thick, even layer. Smooth the top. Put the mold immediately into the freezer and freeze until really firm. Meanwhile, whip the cream until stiff. In a separate bowl, whisk the egg white until it forms soft peaks, then gently whisk in the sugar until glossy and stiff. Fold together the whipped cream, egg white, and strained raspberries, and chill. When the chocolate ice is really firm, spoon the raspberry mixture into the middle of the bombe. Smooth the top, cover with waxed paper or foil, and freeze for at least 2 hours.

About 20 minutes before serving, remove the bombe from the freezer, push a fine skewer through the middle to release the air lock, and run a knife around the inside top edge. Invert onto a chilled plate and briefly wipe the pan with a hot cloth. Squeeze or shake the pan once or twice to see if the bombe will slip out; if not, wipe again with a hot cloth. When it slips out, you may need to neaten the top surface with a small palette knife, and then return to the freezer immediately for at least 20 minutes to firm up again. Serve, cut into slices, with the raspberry sauce. This bombe will keep for 3 to 4 weeks in its pan in the freezer.

Serves 6–8

grand marnier & orange iced soufflé

see variations page 228

This fabulous dessert has a crisp yet melt-in-the-mouth texture. It can almost be eaten straight from the freezer, but it can also sit around in the fridge for a couple of hours.

4 large oranges
1 (1/4-oz.) envelope unflavored gelatin
6 large eggs, separated
1 cup plus 2 tbsp. superfine sugar
4 to 6 tbsp. Grand Marnier

2 tbsp. lemon juice
1 3/4 cups whipping cream, whipped
2 tbsp. water
few stems of red currants

Prepare a 7-inch-wide, deep soufflé dish by wrapping it in a collar of double waxed paper that comes about 2 inches above the rim. Secure the waxed paper with tape. Finely grate the zest of 2 oranges and set aside. Squeeze out enough juice from 2 or 3 of the oranges to make 1 cup of juice. Heat the orange juice and then stir in the gelatin. Set it aside to dissolve or put it in a small bowl over hot water until completely dissolved.

Whisk the egg yolks and 1 cup of the sugar until thick and creamy. Whisk in the orange juice, orange zest, Grand Marnier, and lemon juice. Set aside to cool but don't chill. Whisk the egg whites until stiff. Fold them gently into the cooled orange and egg yolk mixture, followed by the whipped cream, until well incorporated. Spoon into the prepared soufflé dish and freeze for several hours or overnight.

Thinly slice and halve the remaining orange and place in a shallow pan or frying pan with the remaining 2 tablespoons sugar and 2 tablespoons water. Simmer gently until tender, then cook over a high heat until the orange segments begin to caramelize. Cool thoroughly on a sheet of waxed paper.

To serve, carefully remove the paper collar from around the soufflé and put the dish on a serving plate. Arrange the caramelized orange segments on top of the soufflé and add a few stems of fresh red currants.

Serves 8

iced double chocolate mousses

see variations page 229

Irresistible for chocoholics and wicked for dieters — but you could share one if that makes you feel less guilty!

3 to 4 tbsp. very hot milk
1 (1/4-oz.) envelope unflavored gelatin
1 1/2 cups white chocolate chunks
4 tbsp. (1/2 stick) unsalted butter
2 large egg whites
1/2 cup superfine sugar

1/2 cup finely chopped dark chocolate (you want to keep some texture)
1/2 cup heavy cream, lightly whipped
1/2 cup Greek-style yogurt
18 chocolate-covered coffee beans or raisins
1 tsp. unsweetened cocoa powder, sifted

Sprinkle the gelatin onto the hot milk and stir to dissolve. If necessary, microwave for 30 seconds to help it dissolve. Melt the white chocolate and butter gently until smooth. Stir in the dissolved gelatin and set aside to cool, but don't let it firm up again. Whisk the egg whites stiffly, then gradually whisk in the sugar and fold in the dark chocolate.

Carefully fold together the cooled white chocolate, whipped cream, yogurt, and egg whites. Spoon the mixture into 6 individual molds, or one large mold, lined with plastic wrap for easy unmolding. Neatly flatten the tops. Cover and freeze for 1 to 2 hours or overnight.

To serve, loosen the top edges with a small knife. Invert each mold onto a serving plate and wipe with a hot cloth, or gently ease the mousse out with the plastic wrap. Return the mousses to the freezer, until ready to eat. Serve with chocolate-covered coffee beans or raisins and a light sifting of powdered chocolate.

Serves 6

frozen lemon curd cake

see variations page 230

If you love the creaminess of traditional cheesecake and the sharp sweet tang of lemon curd, you will really go for this rich frozen dessert.

1/2 cup (1 stick) unsalted
    butter
1/2 cup superfine sugar
2 large eggs
1 tsp. pure vanilla extract
1 cup all-purpose flour
1 1/2 tsp. baking powder
2 to 4 tbsp. milk

1 1/2 cups good-quality
    lemon curd
for the filling
2 large lemons
1 (1/4-oz.) envelope
    unflavored gelatin
2 cups cream cheese
1 cup superfine sugar

1 cup plain yogurt
2 large egg whites
for the topping
1 recipe caramel (page 14)

Preheat the oven to 375°F (190°C). Beat the butter and sugar together until pale and creamy, then beat in the eggs and vanilla. Gradually stir in the dry ingredients, adding a little milk if the mixture is not a soft, dropping consistency. When well blended, spoon into a nonstick 8-inch-square, loose-bottomed cake pan. Smooth the top and bake for 20 to 25 minutes until evenly risen and just firm to the touch. Let cool in the pan.

Meanwhile, remove some large fine shreds of lemon zest for decoration, and keep covered. Grate the rest of the zest into a mixing bowl. Squeeze the juice into a measuring cup, and add water to make 3/4 cup liquid. Heat this liquid, then sprinkle with the gelatin, and stir until dissolved. Let cool. Put the cottage cheese into the bowl with the lemon zest, add half the sugar, and beat until creamy smooth. Then blend in the cooled gelatin and the yogurt.

In a separate bowl, whisk the egg white until stiff, then fold in the sugar. Fold this mixture into the cottage cheese mixture until smooth. Spread a thick layer of lemon curd over the cake in the pan and then spoon on the cottage cheese mixture. Smooth the top and place in the freezer for 2 hours or until ready to serve.

To serve, carefully remove the cheesecake from the pan and transfer to a serving plate. Cover the top with broken pieces of caramel and the reserved shreds of lemon zest. Serve while still partly frozen. Slice into 12 squares and serve immediately.

Serves 8

pineapple baked alaska

see variations page 231

Most children love the surprise of this dessert—hot meringue with ice-cold ice cream inside. Do use a good firm ice cream, not a soft scoop, to make sure the center doesn't soften too quickly.

1 6 to 8-oz. piece store-bought ginger cake
6 slices ripe, peeled pineapple
3 cups tutti-frutti gelato (page 62), softening

3 large egg whites
3/4 cup superfine sugar
few pieces of fresh pineapple, to decorate

Slice the cake into 2 thick pieces and arrange in a square or circle on a sheet of reusable pan liner on a baking pan, so you can transfer it easily to a serving dish later.

Cut the 6 pineapple slices into triangles or quarters, over the cake to catch any drips. Arrange the pineapple pieces on top of the cake, and then top with the gelato. Immediately put the pan in the freezer to refreeze the gelato, if it has softened too much.

Meanwhile, whisk the egg whites until very stiff, then whisk in the sugar gradually until the mixture becomes stiff and glossy. Spread the meringue mixture evenly all over the gelato and return to the freezer. This can be frozen for a couple of days, if desired.

When ready to serve, heat the oven to 450°F (230°C). Put the baking pan into the hot oven for only 5 to 7 minutes, or until turning golden all over. Transfer to a serving dish and serve immediately, decorated with a few pieces of fresh pineapple.

Serves 6–8

iced strawberry pavlova roll

see variations page 232

Melt-in-the-mouth meringue rolled around strawberry sorbet and whipped cream is a star dessert and not as complicated as it looks.

2 tsp. cornstarch	1 1/2 cups strawberry sorbet (page 78)
1 cup superfine sugar	1/2 cup heavy cream
4 egg whites, at room temperature	confectioners' sugar, fresh strawberries, and
confectioners' sugar, sifted	mint leaves, to decorate

Line a 12 x 9-in. jelly-roll pan with a nonstick baking liner or waxed paper, cut to fit. Sift the cornstarch and blend evenly with the superfine sugar. Whisk the egg whites until they form firm peaks but are not dry and crumbly. Then whisk in the sugar-cornstarch mixture gradually until stiff and glossy. Spoon into the prepared pan and flatten the top out. Place in a cold oven and turn it to 300°F (150°C). Cook for 1 hour until the top is crisp but the meringue still feels springy (if it appears to be coloring early in the cooking, reduce the temperature so it does not turn brown). Turn out immediately onto a double sheet of waxed paper that has been sprinkled with sifted confectioners' sugar, and let cool.

Meanwhile, soften the sorbet and whip the cream. When the meringue has cooled, carefully and quickly spread it with the sorbet and then with the whipped cream. Roll up, using the paper as a support, and wrap lightly in foil. Return to the freezer. Freeze for about 1 hour (or up to several days) before serving, sprinkled with more confectioners' sugar and topped with fresh strawberries and mint.

Serves 6–8

iced raspberry & peach trifle

see variations page 233

You can't get quicker than this for a pretty, colorful, and tasty party dessert.

4 pieces of pound cake, chopped
4 to 8 tbsp. sherry or Marsala
7 to 8 tbsp. raspberry jelly
1 cup fresh or frozen raspberries

2 firm ripe peaches, peeled and sliced
4 scoops vanilla ice cream, softening
1 cup whipped heavy cream
fresh raspberries and peach slices, to decorate

Crumble the cake into the base of 4 glass serving dishes or glasses. Sprinkle the sherry or Marsala evenly over the cake.

Combine the jelly and raspberries, then spoon over the cake. Top with the sliced peaches.

Spread the softening ice cream over the peaches. Spread with the whipped cream and freeze for up to 1 hour before serving.

When ready to serve, top with a few pieces of fresh fruit.

Serves 4

frozen macaroon terrine

see base recipe page 209

pistachio terrine
Prepare the basic recipe, coating with a pistachio praline (page 14).

tiramisu terrine
Prepare the basic recipe, replacing the heavy cream with ricotta and the Amaretto with coffee liqueur. Soak the crushed macaroons in the liqueur before adding them. Coat the terrine with a fine shower of unsweetened cocoa powder instead of the crushed praline.

chocolate terrine
When preparing the basic recipe, replace the macaroons with fine chocolate cake crumbs. Coat the frozen terrine with grated dark chocolate instead of crushed praline.

marbled fudge terrine
Prepare the basic recipe, omitting the macaroons and the Amaretto. Swirl 1/2 cup chocolate fudge sauce (page 13) through the filling before freezing. Instead of the crushed praline, coat the frozen terrine with finely crushed ginger cookies or another favorite cookie.

variations

chocolate & cherry ice cream gateau

see base recipe page 210

chocolate & toffee apple ice cream gateau
Prepare the basic recipe, replacing the cherry and cranberry filling with
2 finely chopped apples mixed with 1/2 cup toffee sauce (page 13). Decorate
with whipped cream, a few wedges of apple, and a drizzle of toffee sauce.

chocolate & raspberry ice cream gateau
Prepare the basic recipe, replacing the cherries with raspberries. Omit the
brown sugar and cranberry juice, but use a little raspberry juice to moisten the
cake layers. Decorate with whipped cream, raspberries, and chocolate curls.

chocolate, rum & raisin ice cream gateau
Prepare the basic recipe, replacing the vanilla gelato with rum & raisin ice
cream (page 31) and the cherry filling with 2 1/2 sliced bananas mashed with
half the brown sugar. Omit the cranberry juice, but use a little rum or fruit
juice to moisten the cake layers. Decorate with whipped cream, slices of the
remaining half banana, and a few chocolate curls.

chocolate & mango ice cream gateau
Prepare the basic recipe, replacing the gelato with mango sorbet (page 82) and
the cherries with sliced mangoes or peaches. Omit the brown sugar and
cranberry juice. Use a little orange or peach juice to moisten the cake layers.
Decorate with whipped cream, a few mango pieces, and chocolate curls.

variations

chocolate bombe

see base recipe page 213

banoffee bombe
Prepare the basic recipe, but replace the raspberries in the filling with
bananas mashed with 1 tablespoon lemon juice. Serve with chocolate sauce
(page 13).

coffee cream bombe
When preparing the basic recipe, replace the raspberries in the filling with
6 tablespoons coffee syrup (page 12) and 1/4 cup toasted sliced almonds.
Serve with heavy cream or a coffee liqueur poured on top instead of
raspberry sauce.

vanilla truffle bombe
Prepare the basic recipe, using luxury vanilla gelato (page 53) for the outer
layer. For the filling, replace the raspberries with 6 tablespoons chocolate
sauce (page 13) and 2 tablespoons brandy. Serve with hot chocolate sauce.

nesselrode bombe
Prepare the basic recipe, but replace the raspberries in the filling with
canned chestnut purée, mixed with 1 tablespoon each chopped candied
ginger and candied citrus peel. Omit the raspberry sauce.

variations

grand marnier & orange iced soufflé

see base recipe page 214

grand marnier, orange & chocolate iced soufflé
Prepare the basic recipe, but stir in 1/2 cup dark chocolate chips or grated chocolate before spooning into the soufflé dish.

orange & ginger iced soufflé
Prepare the basic recipe, replacing the Grand Marnier with ginger syrup. Top with crystallized (candied) chopped ginger instead of orange segments and red currants.

pink grapefruit & hazelnut iced soufflé
Prepare the basic recipe, replacing the 4 oranges with 2 pink grapefruits. Remove the rind from 1 grapefruit in long shreds and set aside for later. Remove the rind from the other grapefruit with as much juice as necessary and continue following the basic recipe. Stir in 1/2 cup crushed toasted hazelnuts before spooning into the soufflé dish. While the soufflé is chilling, simmer the shredded rind with the sugar and water until caramelized. Top the soufflé with a few cracked hazelnuts and the candied grapefruit rind.

pink grapefruit & cassis iced soufflé
Prepare the basic recipe, replacing the 4 oranges with 2 pink grapefruits (prepared as in the variation above) and the Grand Marnier with cassis or black currant liqueur. Use a few black currants or blackberries on top along with the candied grapefruit rind.

variations

iced double chocolate mousses

see base recipe page 217

iced chocolate & blueberry mousses
Prepare the basic recipe, replacing the chopped dark chocolate with fresh blueberries, lightly crushed to release just a little juice and color. Decorate with just a few fresh berries.

iced chocolate & nougat mousses
When preparing the basic recipe, replace the chopped dark chocolate with broken-up pieces of nougat.

iced chocolate & berry mousses
Prepare the basic recipe, replacing the chopped dark chocolate with freeze-dried berries. Decorate with a few fresh berries.

iced chocolate liqueur mousses
Prepare the basic recipe, omitting the chopped dark chocolate. Add 4 tablespoons of a chilled liqueur of your choice — hazelnut, mint, coffee, or fruit — to the mixture before freezing. Serve simply with powdered chocolate.

iced chocolate & lime mousses
Prepare the mousses as described, omitting the chopped dark chocolate. Stir into the mixture the finely grated zest and the juice of 1 lime before freezing. Serve with a little more grated lime zest.

variations

frozen lemon curd cake

see base recipe page 218

frozen strawberry lemon cake
Prepare the basic recipe, using strawberry jelly instead of lemon curd and strawberry yogurt instead of plain yogurt. Top with sliced strawberries and whipped cream instead of caramel pieces.

frozen tangerine marmalade cake
When preparing the basic recipe, use marmalade instead of lemon curd and 3 or 4 tangerines instead of the 2 lemons.

frozen plum ginger cake
Prepare the basic recipe, using plum jelly instead of lemon curd and adding 1/2 cup finely chopped crystallized or candied ginger to the filling. Top with sliced plums and more candied ginger instead of caramel pieces.

frozen chocolate chestnut cake
Prepare the basic recipe, replacing 1 tablespoon flour in the cake with 1 tablespoon unsweetened powdered cocoa. When making the filling, omit the lemon rind and the yogurt and blend in 1 cup well-creamed, canned chestnut purée. Instead of the lemon curd, spread the cake with a chocolate spread. Top with grated chocolate and whipped cream instead of caramel pieces.

pineapple baked alaska

see base recipe page 221

banana baked alaska
When preparing the basic recipe, replace the tutti-frutti gelato with banana custard ice cream (page 140) and the pineapple with 2 sliced large bananas. Serve decorated with banana chips.

mango & lime baked alaska
Prepare the basic recipe, replacing the tutti-frutti gelato with lime gelato (page 72) and the pineapple with fresh mango. Serve decorated with lime leaves or finely grated lime zest.

pear & almond baked alaska
Prepare the basic recipe using pound cake, vanilla ice cream, and sliced pears. Serve decorated with toasted almonds.

mixed citrus baked alaska
Prepare the basic recipe using carrot cake, vanilla ice cream, and segments of tangerines, satsumas, mandarins, or clementines. Serve decorated with candied orange peel.

strawberry baked alaska
Prepare the basic recipe, using pound cake instead of ginger cake and halved fresh strawberries instead of pineapple. Serve decorated with fresh strawberries.

variations

iced strawberry pavlova roll

see base recipe page 222

iced passion fruit ripple roll
Prepare the basic recipe, but use vanilla ice cream instead of the strawberry
sorbet, omit the whipped cream, and drizzle the vanilla ice cream with the
pulp of 2 passion fruit before rolling up. Serve with a little more passion
fruit pulp spooned evenly on top instead of strawberries and mint.

iced chocolate marshmallow roll
Prepare the basic recipe, using bitter chocolate gelato (page 57) instead of
strawberry sorbet. Sprinkle with chopped marshmallows before rolling up.
Serve topped with chocolate flakes or curls instead of strawberries and mint.

iced coffee & nut roll
When preparing the basic recipe, use coffee gelato (page 63) instead of the
strawberry sorbet. Sprinkle with 1/2 cup chopped nuts before rolling up.
Serve drizzled with toffee sauce (page 13) instead of decorating with
strawberries and mint.

iced hazelnut & lemon roll
Make the basic recipe, adding 1/4 cup crushed toasted hazelnuts to the
meringue mixture before cooking. Replace the strawberry sorbet with lemon
gelato (page 61). Serve sprinkled with more toasted nuts and confectioners'
sugar instead of strawberries and mint.

iced raspberry & peach trifle

see base recipe page 224

iced burnt-sugar raspberry trifle
Prepare the basic recipe, but use heatproof dishes and omit the peaches. Top the whipped cream with a layer of demerara sugar. Place the dishes under the broiler until the sugar is lightly browned and caramelized. Cool slightly before freezing. To serve, top with a few raspberries.

iced pear & quince trifle
When preparing the basic recipe, replace the raspberry jelly with quince jelly and the raspberries and peaches with 2 to 3 ripe pears, peeled and sliced. Top with more pear slices.

iced chocolate & orange trifle
Prepare the basic recipe, replacing the pound cake with chocolate cake, the raspberry jelly with orange jelly (or use Jello), the raspberries and peaches with 2 to 3 peeled and sliced oranges, and the vanilla ice cream with bitter chocolate gelato (page 57). Top with grated chocolate.

iced hawaiian trifle
Prepare the basic recipe but replace the pound cake with a favorite coffee cake, the raspberry jelly with lime jelly (or use Jello), and the peaches and raspberries with mango, papaya, pineapple, or other tropical fruits. Use coffee gelato (page 63) and top with shredded toasted coconut.

dairy-free ice creams

If you think ice cream has to be made with milk, eggs, or cream, think again. Numerous delicious nondairy alternatives—rice, oat, bean, and nut-based milks and yogurts; and fruits like bananas—can make a perfect ice cream base.

ginger tofu ice cream with caramelized oranges

see variations page 250

Silken (smooth) tofu makes a lovely, creamy ice cream that everyone will enjoy, regardless of their diet.

1 cup silken tofu
1 cup soy milk
1/2 cup pure maple syrup
2 tsp. ground ginger
1/4 cup chopped crystallized or candied ginger
1 tsp. pure vanilla extract

finely grated zest and juice of 1 large orange
for the caramelized oranges
2 large oranges
1/2 cup sugar
4 tbsp. water

Gently mix all the ice cream ingredients together into a smooth blend. Spoon into an ice cream maker and churn following the manufacturer's directions, or transfer to a freezer container and follow the hand-mixing instructions on page 8. When almost firm, freeze in a freezer container for 15 to 20 minutes before serving. The ice cream can be frozen for up to 1 month, allowing 10 or 15 minutes to soften before serving.

Remove strips of zest from the 2 large oranges and set aside, then remove and discard any remaining rind and the white pith. Cut the oranges into slices and set aside. Cut the zest into fine strips and place in a small saucepan with the sugar and water. Heat until the sugar has dissolved, and then simmer until the mixture forms a golden syrup. Remove from the heat immediately and add the sliced oranges. Return to the heat and cook gently for about 5 minutes, until the slices are well softened, chill. Serve the tofu ice cream with slices of caramelized oranges and a little of the syrup drizzled on top.

Serves 4

coconut ice with lime

see variations page 251

Coconut milk makes a great base for an ice cream, but you can enrich it by using the thicker (higher fat content, of course!) coconut cream. The coconut flavor is great with the sharp tang of limes.

2 cups coconut milk, chilled
finely grated zest and juice of 3 limes
4 tbsp. honey, or to taste
dried coconut, toasted, to decorate

Blend all the ingredients together in a food processor until well mixed. Place in an ice cream maker and process according to the manufacturer's directions, or put into a freezer container and freeze using the hand-mixing method (page 8) until almost firm.

Transfer to a freezer container and freeze until firm enough to serve, or cover and freeze for up to 3 months. Serve topped with toasted coconut.

Makes 3 cups

creamy banana roll

see variations page 252

This ice cream roll is rich with the sweet taste of bananas.

6 ripe bananas
2 cups soy milk
6 tbsp. pure maple syrup
2 tsp. pure vanilla extract

3 tbsp. toasted sesame seeds
2 to 3 tbsp. unsweetened cocoa powder, sifted
flakes or curls of chocolate, to decorate
1/2 recipe chocolate sauce (page 13)

Freeze the bananas in their skins for about 2 hours.

Peel, slice, and process the bananas in a food processor with the soy milk, maple syrup, vanilla, and sesame seeds until well blended. Spoon into a foil-lined baking sheet, spread out evenly, and freeze for 1 hour. Remove when it is still slightly soft. Then roll up (in jelly-roll style) into a cylinder, covering with a second layer of foil, and twisting the ends tightly to give the roll a good neat shape. Freeze for another hour until really firm.

To serve, unwrap the roll on a flat surface and shower all over with the cocoa powder. Transfer to a serving dish and decorate with chocolate curls, or drizzle with chocolate sauce. Serve sliced, with more chocolate sauce.

Serves 8

frozen yogurt with rosemary and candied fruit

see variations page 253

The delicate herbal flavor of rosemary and lightly floral aroma of candied violets makes for a wonderfully aromatic, gently scented ice.

1 tsp. fresh rosemary leaves
1/2 cup confectioners' sugar
1/2 cup candied orange and lemon peel

2 cups soy or nondairy yogurt
2 tbsp. candied violets

Finely chop the rosemary leaves and mix with the confectioners' sugar. Let stand for at least an hour, and preferably overnight.

Finely chop the candied peel (even if it is already chopped). Mix the yogurt with the candied peel and candied violets in a large bowl. Sift the confectioners' sugar over the bowl, then stir it in. Divide the mixture between 8 ramekins or small molds. Put into the freezer and leave for 2–3 hours.

Shortly before serving, stand the molds briefly in boiling water, then turn the frozen yogurt out onto plates. If you wish, serve garnished with rosemary sprigs and slices of fresh fruit.

Serves 8

frozen chocolate surprise

see variations page 254

This Japanese-inspired vegan recipe for chocolate ice cream is both good for you and utterly delicious.

1 cup anko or adzuki beans, soaked overnight
    (or 14-oz. can azuki beans)
2 cups dark brown sugar
2 cups water

4 tbsp. carob powder
2 cups rice milk
1 cup rice or soy yogurt
sliced fresh fruit, to serve

Drain the soaked beans and place them in a large pan covered with water. Bring to a boil and simmer for 1 hour or until they begin to soften. Drain and return to the pan with the brown sugar and 2 cups water. Cook, uncovered, over moderate heat until really tender and much of the liquid has reduced. Cool.

(If using canned adzuki beans, drain and rinse in fresh water, then simmer with the brown sugar and 1 cup water until really tender and much of the liquid has reduced. Cool.)

Blend the beans in a processor with enough of their cooking liquid to make a soft purée. Then blend in the carob powder, rice milk, and yogurt. Blend until really smooth. Transfer to an ice cream maker and churn following the manufacturer's instructions, or transfer to a freezer container and follow the hand-mixing directions on page 8. If using an ice cream maker, stop churning when it is almost firm, transfer to a freezer container, and leave in the freezer for 15 minutes before serving, or until required. When ready to serve, remove from the freezer and leave for 15 minutes to soften. Serve with sliced fresh fruit.

Makes 5 cups

grape sorbet

see variations page 255

Sweet muscat grapes have a wonderful perfume and flavor that create a great sorbet, especially when enhanced with a little sweet muscat wine.

2 cups loose muscat grapes (or any sweet green
    or red grapes)
1 cup sugar syrup (page 11)
finely grated zest and juice of 1 lemon

1 cup muscat or any favorite dessert wine, plus
    more to serve
1 cup rice, soy, or oat milk

Halve the grapes and remove any seeds. In a food processor, blend the grapes with the sugar syrup to a fine purée. Add the remaining ingredients and blend smooth.

Churn in an ice cream maker according to the manufacturer's directions, or pour into a freezer container and follow the hand-mixing directions (page 8). When almost firm, freeze in a freezer container until firm or until required.

Serve scooped into tiny bowls or glasses and drizzle on a little more muscat or dessert wine.

Makes 5 cups

frozen raspberry soy cups

see variations page 256

These raspberry cups will make a pretty end to any special meal.

1 (1/4-oz.) envelope unflavored gelatin
3 tbsp. lemon juice
2 cups fresh raspberries
1/2 cup superfine sugar
2 cups raspberry soy yogurt

1 tsp. pure vanilla extract
6 small chocolate cups (page 15)
4 tbsp. soy cream, whipped
6 fresh raspberries

Dissolve the gelatin in a small pan with the lemon juice over a gentle heat, or microwave in 30-second bursts. Cool.

In a food processor, blend the raspberries with the sugar, soy yogurt, and vanilla to a smooth purée. Set aside 3 tablespoons. of the purée for the topping. Mix the dissolved gelatin into the remaining purée. Churn the mixture in an ice cream maker following the manufacturer's directions, or spoon into a freezer container and freeze using the hand-mixing method (page 8) until just spoonable. Spoon the raspberry mixture into individual chocolate cups and freeze for 1 to 2 hours.

Strain the reserved purée, then fold in the whipped cream. Whip again if necessary to stiffen slightly, then spoon into a small piping bag fitted with a fluted nozzle. Pipe swirls of this raspberry cream on top of the raspberry cups and return to the freezer until ready to serve. Serve these cups when iced but not frozen hard. If the cups do become frozen solid, allow about 20 minutes at room temperature before serving. Top each serving with a fresh raspberry.

Makes 6

frozen date & oatmeal energy bars

see variations page 257

This unusual version of an ice cream never gets really hard, so these power-packed snack pieces can be eaten straight from the freezer any time.

2 cups pitted dates
1/2 cup orange juice
1 tsp. pure vanilla extract
1/2 cup water
1 cup rice, oat, or soy milk, chilled

2 cups unsweetened muesli or granola
4 tbsp. demerara sugar
4 tbsp. light corn syrup
4 tbsp. lightly crushed praline (page 14)

Cook the dates with the orange juice, vanilla, and water to a soft puréed consistency. Set aside until just cooled. Blend in the milk, then put into a freezer container to freeze until firm but spreadable.

Meanwhile, preheat the oven to 375°F (190°C). Mix the muesli with the sugar, spread out on a baking sheet, and bake for about 15 minutes until golden and crunchy. Put into a bowl and mix with the corn syrup. Spread into a 9-inch square or 9 x 12-inch oblong pan or container. Chill until the date mixture is ready.

Spread the date ice over the muesli base, then sprinkle with the crushed praline, and freeze for 1 hour. Cut into fingers or squares and return to the freezer until really firm. These can be frozen, well-wrapped, for up to 3 months.

Makes about 20 pieces

ginger tofu ice cream with caramelized oranges

see base recipe page 235

citrus tofu ice
Prepare the basic ice cream recipe, replacing the ground ginger with
the finely grated zest of 1 lime, 1 lemon, and 1 orange, and the candied
ginger with candied citrus peel.

pineapple tofu ice
When preparing the ice cream, omit the ground ginger and replace
the candied ginger with candied pineapple. Serve with pineapple sauce
(page 14) instead of the caramelized oranges.

ginger & cherry tofu ice
Prepare the basic recipe, replacing the candied ginger with chopped
candied cherries. Serve with a shot of maraschino liqueur and some fresh
cherries instead of the caramelized oranges.

spiced seeded tofu ice
Prepare the basic recipe, replacing the ground ginger with allspice and
the candied ginger with 1/8 cup toasted and cooled mixed seeds (such
as sesame, sunflower, or pumpkin seeds). Serve with the caramelized
oranges or a little soy cream.

coconut ice with lime

see base recipe page 236

coconut ice with lime & mint

Prepare the basic recipe, adding 2 tablespoons chopped fresh mint before churning or freezing. Serve with sprigs of fresh mint instead of coconut.

coconut ice with tangerine

Make this ice cream by replacing the limes with 3 firm tangerines or clementines.

coconut ice with figs

When preparing the basic recipe, replace the limes with the flesh of 5 large, very ripe purple figs (scooped out of their skins).

coconut ice with pomegranate

Prepare the basic recipe, replacing the limes with the seeds of half a pomegranate and adding 4 tablespoons pomegranate syrup. Serve topped with the remaining seeds and a few drops of syrup.

coconut ice with pineapple

Prepare the basic recipe, replacing the limes with 1 cup fresh pineapple purée.

variations

creamy banana roll

see base recipe page 239

creamy banana & coffee roll
Prepare the basic recipe, adding 4 tablespoons coffee syrup (page 12).
Serve with coffee syrup or coffee liqueur instead of chocolate sauce.

creamy banana & toffee roll
Prepare the basic recipe, replacing the maple syrup with toffee sauce
(page 13). Serve with more toffee sauce.

creamy banana & pineapple roll
When preparing the basic recipe, replace 2 bananas with 1 cup chopped
fresh pineapple and serve with pineapple sauce (page 14).

creamy banana & pecan roll
Prepare the basic recipe, replacing the sesame seeds with 6 tablespoons
roughly chopped toasted pecans. Replace the cocoa powder with
6 tablespoons very finely chopped toasted pecans and serve with
chocolate or toffee sauce (page 13).

variations

frozen yogurt with rosemary & candied fruit

see base recipe page 240

frozen mint yogurt

Prepare the basic recipe, omitting the rosemary, confectioners' sugar, candied peel, and candied violets. Stir 2 tablespoons finely chopped fresh mint leaves into the yogurt just before freezing. There's no need to mix the mint into the sugar and leave overnight.

frozen blueberry yogurt

When preparing the basic recipe, omit the rosemary, confectioners' sugar, candied peel, and candied violets. Stir 1/2 cup fresh blueberries into the yogurt just before freezing.

frozen yogurt with mixed nuts

Prepare the basic recipe, omitting the rosemary, confectioners' sugar, candied peel, and candied violets. Stir 1/3 cup mixed chopped nuts (hazelnuts, walnuts, almonds, etc.) into the yogurt just before freezing.

frozen yogurt with dried cranberries

Prepare the basic recipe, omitting the rosemary, confectioners' sugar, candied peel, and candied violets. Stir 1/2 cup dried cranberries into the yogurt just before freezing.

variations

frozen chocolate surprise

see base recipe page 243

frozen cinnamon chocolate surprise
Follow the basic recipe, adding 2 to 3 teaspoons ground cinnamon.

frozen mocha surprise
Prepare the basic recipe, adding 4 tablespoons coffee syrup (page 12) and serve with a little more syrup or coffee liqueur poured on top.

frozen chile-chocolate surprise
When preparing the basic recipe, add 1/2 to 1 teaspoon chili powder (according to your taste).

frozen nutty chocolate surprise
Prepare the basic recipe, stirring in 4 tablespoons chopped walnuts just before the final freezing.

grape sorbet

see base recipe page 244

pear sorbet
Prepare the basic recipe, replacing the grapes with 2 large ripe sweet pears, peeled and chopped. Serve with a shot of a pear liqueur.

currant sorbet
Replace the grapes of the basic recipe with black, red, or white currants, with extra sugar syrup added to taste. Serve with a shot of cassis.

lychee sorbet
Prepare the basic recipe, replacing the grapes with 2 (12-oz.) cans of pitted lychees, drained, and replace the sugar syrup with 1 cup of the lychee syrup. Add 3 tablespoons light corn syrup.

cape gooseberry sorbet
Prepare the basic recipe, replacing the grapes with cape gooseberries without their paper cases. Serve topped with a gooseberry in its paper case.

cranberry sorbet
Prepare the basic recipe, replacing grapes with cranberries and muscat with cassis. Cook the cranberries in the sugar syrup for 5 to 10 minutes or until they have opened, then push through a sieve and continue with the recipe.

variations

frozen raspberry soy cups

see base recipe page 247

summer fruit soy cups
Follow the basic recipe, replacing the raspberries with fresh or frozen and defrosted summer fruits. Use a yogurt flavor that suits best.

cranberry soy cups
When preparing the basic recipe, replace the raspberries with fresh or frozen (and defrosted) cranberries, adding extra sugar to taste. Use peach or apricot yogurt instead of raspberry yogurt.

blueberry soy cups
Prepare the basic recipe, replacing the raspberries with blueberries and the raspberry yogurt with blueberry or cherry yogurt.

cherry soy cups
Replace the raspberries of basic recipe with pitted chopped cherries and the raspberry yogurt with cherry or blueberry yogurt.

creamy strawberry cups
If you don't need a dairy-free dessert, prepare the basic recipe with strawberry dairy yogurt instead of the soy yogurt and dairy cream instead of the soy cream. Top with a small strawberry instead of a raspberry.

variations

frozen date & oatmeal energy bars

see base recipe page 248

frozen date & cornflake bars
Prepare the basic recipe, replacing the muesli with 3 cups lightly crushed cornflakes. Do not cook in the oven, but simply mix with warmed syrup. Continue as described.

frozen fig & oatmeal energy bars
When preparing the basic recipe, replace the dates with figs.

frozen prune & oatmeal energy bars
Prepare the basic recipe but replace the dates with dried pitted prunes.

frozen chestnut energy bars
Prepare the basic recipe, replacing the dates with 2 cups canned chestnut purée (there's no need to cook it) and adding 2 to 3 tablespoons maple or light corn syrup to sweeten as desired.

frozen pumpkin & oatmeal energy bars
Prepare the basic recipe, replacing the dates with 2 cups canned pumpkin (there's no need to cook it) and adding 4 tablespoons maple syrup or light corn syrup to sweeten as desired.

low-fat &
sugar-free ices

If you're an ice cream addict, it's so hard to keep to
a diet. But perhaps some of these delicious, lower-
calorie alternatives can tempt you away from the
richer ones at the beginning of the book!

apricot whip

see variations page 274

This delicious ice cream blends the rich sweetness of dried apricots with the light tang of cream cheese — a winner on any diet!

2 cups dried apricots (Hunza apricots
    recommended, if available)
1 cup water
1 cup orange juice
2 tsp. pure vanilla extract

1 tsp. almond extract
4 tbsp. honey or preferred sweetener
1 cup fat-free cream cheese
1 cup fat-free milk
2 tbsp. toasted sliced almonds, to decorate

Simmer the apricots in a small saucepan with the water and orange juice until really soft (20 to 30 minutes). Blend in a food processor until very smooth. Add the vanilla and almond extracts, honey, cream cheese, and milk. Blend again until smooth. Chill.

Transfer the chilled mixture to an ice cream maker and churn following the manufacturer's directions, or freeze using the hand-mixing method (page 8). When firm, leave in the freezer until ready to serve. Decorate ice cream with the toasted almonds.

The ice cream can be frozen for up to 3 months. Remove from the freezer 15 minutes before serving to soften slightly.

Makes about 1 1/2 pints

zingy citrus yogurt ice

see variations page 275

This is a seriously tangy citrus ice, but you can add more sweetener or honey if you wish.

1 tsp. finely grated citrus zest
1 cup mixed citrus juice (for instance 1 orange,
    1 lemon, and 1 lime)

2 tbsp. sweetener (or to taste)
2 cups fat-free plain yogurt
1 egg white

Mix the zest, juice, sweetener, and yogurt together. Whisk the egg white until stiff, then whisk in the juice mixture.

Pour into an ice cream maker and churn following the manufacturer's directions, or pour into a freezer container and freeze using the hand-mixing instructions on page 8. When firm, leave in the freezer until ready to serve.

The ice can be frozen for up to 3 months. Remove from the freezer 10 to 15 minutes before serving to soften slightly.

Makes 1 1/4 pints

passion fruit ice milk

see variations page 276

This delicately flavored ice milk will fit into any diet. It's great after a special dinner too!

1 (1/4-oz.) envelope unflavored gelatin
juice of 1 lemon
1 cup passion fruit pulp (about 4 large fruit)
1 1/2 cups fat-free milk

1 tsp. pure vanilla extract
1 to 2 tbsp. honey
flesh of 1 passion fruit, to serve
slices of ripe peach, to serve

Dissolve the gelatin in the lemon juice in a small bowl set over hot water. When dissolved, put aside to cool slightly.

Scoop the passion fruit pulp into a bowl. Whisk in the milk, vanilla, and honey, along with the cooled gelatin. Spoon into small serving dishes or ramekins and chill until set.

Place the dishes in the freezer for 1 hour before serving. To serve, top with a little extra passion fruit and peach slices. You may also turn the ices out onto a larger serving dish, if you wish. Just run a warm knife around the inside rim of the dish before inverting onto a serving dish.

Serves 4–6

ricotta ice with roasted figs

see variations page 277

If you feel low-fat ricotta is too high-fat for you, try using virtually fat-free fromage frais instead (try a specialty gourmet shop; it's not readily available).

12 ripe purple figs
6 tbsp. orange blossom honey
1 cup low-fat ricotta

1/2 cup fat-free milk
1 tsp. pure vanilla extract
finely grated zest and juice of 1 orange

Preheat the oven to 425°F (220°C). Cut the figs into quarters but not all the way through. Arrange, quite tightly packed, in an ovenproof dish and drizzle with the honey. Roast in the top of the oven for about 10 minutes, basting once, until they just begin to brown. Remove from the oven and chill as quickly as possible.

Set aside the 4 firmest or nicest figs, with a little of the juice from the dish, to serve later. Scoop the flesh of the rest of the figs into a bowl with the rest of the juice, and blend to a smooth purée. Add the remaining ingredients and blend until smooth.

Transfer the mixture to an ice cream maker and churn according to the manufacturer's directions, or put into a freezer container and freeze using the hand-mixing method (page 8). When firm, freeze until ready to serve. Top each serving with a roasted fig and a drizzle of the juices.

Makes about 1 pint

frosty summer pudding

see variations page 278

Summer pudding is a traditional English dish in which all the wonderful summer berries and currants are packed into a bread casing that absorbs all their sweet juices and turns deep red. This is a frozen, very low-calorie variation.

1 cup fresh breadcrumbs (from day-old white bread)
1 to 2 tbsp. demerara sugar, or to taste
1 lb. frozen summer fruits (such as blackberries, raspberries, strawberries, red and black currants, and cherries)

2 tsp. allspice
frozen or fresh berries, to serve
fresh mint leaves, to serve
low-fat crème fraîche or fromage frais, to serve

Preheat the oven to 375°F (190°C). Line a 2-pint ring mold with plastic wrap and place in the freezer. Place the breadcrumbs on a baking pan with the sugar. Roast in the preheated oven until golden and crispy, stirring once or twice so they are thoroughly crisp. Set aside until completely cooled.

In a food processor, whiz the frozen fruits until well blended and pulpy but not softened. Quickly stir in the toasted breadcrumbs and the allspice. Spoon into the cold ring mold. Smooth the top, cover, and freeze until firm or until ready to serve.

To serve, invert onto a serving plate, remove the plastic wrap, and top with berries and a few fresh mint leaves. Serve immediately with low-fat crème fraîche or fromage frais. This dessert can be kept in the freezer (in or out of the ring mold) for 3 or 4 months, covered with plastic wrap and foil. Remove from the freezer about 15 minutes before serving.

Serves 6–8

frozen banana mango smoothie

see variations page 279

The perfect healthy breakfast on a really hot weekend morning.

2 bananas
1 large or 2 small really ripe mangoes, peeled
    and roughly cut (about 2 cups)
1 cup orange juice

juice of 1/2 lemon
1 cup plain low-fat yogurt
honey or sweetener to taste
extra mango slices, to decorate

Freeze the bananas and the chopped mangoes for 1 to 2 hours or until frozen solid.
Freeze 2 or 3 tall glasses.

When you are ready to serve, peel the bananas and cut them into chunks, setting aside
a couple of slices for garnishing. Quickly blend the frozen bananas and cut-up mangoes
to a pulp, gradually adding all the other ingredients until well blended but still frozen.

Fill the iced glasses and top with a slice of banana or mango or any other fruit.

Serve immediately.

Serves 2–3

iced margarita

see variations page 280

This classic cocktail mix is served frozen, not unlike a snow cone — and very definitely one for adults!

1/2 cup gold tequila
1/2 cup fresh lime juice
1 to 2 tbsp. fine salt

1 cup finely crushed ice
1 slice lime, halved

Put 2 margarita glasses in the freezer for at least 1 hour. Mix the tequila and lime juice and place in the freezer.

Put the salt onto a shallow plate. When ready to serve, dip the rim of the chilled glasses in the salt (because the glasses are cold, the salt will stick to the rim).

Fill the glasses with the crushed ice and then pour in the tequila–lime juice mixture. Serve immediately with the piece of lime.

Serves 2

buck's fizz granita

see variations page 281

Buck's fizz, a delicious cocktail made with equal parts of orange juice and champagne or sparkling white wine, becomes a gorgeous granita when made with blood orange juice and frozen. If you want, try diluting the granita with seltzer, champagne, or even sparkling cider for parties and special occasions.

2 cups blood orange juice
2 cups Prosecco, sparkling white wine, or champagne
   (dry or sweet, according to taste)
1 to 2 tbsp. sweetener or to taste

Chill 6 tall champagne glasses or another tall glass for as long as possible.

Mix the ingredients together and freeze for several hours without stirring, until frozen hard. Scrape with a large fork into a granular mixture and return to the freezer until ready to serve.

Fill the iced glasses with the granita and serve immediately, with a teaspoon, or top off the glasses with additional Prosecco or another sparkling beverage and serve quickly.

Serves 6

variations

apricot whip

see base recipe page 259

prune whip
When preparing the basic recipe, replace the apricots with pitted dried prunes.

pumpkin whip
Prepare the basic recipe, replacing the apricots with canned or cooked pumpkin. Omit the water and the cooking step. Serve with toasted pumpkin seeds instead of almonds.

apple whip
Prepare the basic recipe, replacing the apricots with dried apples (or, if you prefer to use fresh apples, cook 2 sweet apples, peeled and cored, with only 1/2 cup water).

quince whip
Replace the apricots of the basic recipe with 2 cups peeled and chopped fresh quinces

zingy citrus yogurt ice

see base recipe page 260

orange yogurt ice
Prepare the basic recipe using only orange zest and juice and adding
3 tablespoons light rum.

blueberry yogurt ice
Prepare the basic recipe but replace the zest and juice with 1 cup blueberries,
blended to a purée.

greek lemon & honey yogurt ice
Prepare the basic recipe using only lemon zest and juice. Add honey to taste
and replace the yogurt with low-fat, thick Greek-style yogurt.

blood orange yogurt ice
Prepare the basic recipe, using only blood orange zest and juice.

chunky pineapple yogurt ice
Replace the citrus zest and juice of the basic recipe with 1 cup chopped ripe
pineapple, blended to a purée.

variations

passion fruit ice milk

see base recipe page 263

passion fruit & peach ice milk
Prepare the basic recipe, replacing 2 passion fruit with 1 very ripe peeled, pitted, and puréed peach.

lemon–lime ice milk
Replace the passion fruit of the basic recipe with 1 cup mixed lemon and lime juice and add more honey or sweetener to taste.

coffee ice milk
When preparing the basic recipe, dissolve the gelatin in 4 tablespoons water and replace the passion fruit with 1 cup espresso. Add honey or sweetener to taste. Top with crushed roasted nuts instead of the fruit.

pear ice milk
Prepare the basic recipe, replacing the passion fruit with 1 cup peeled, cored, and puréed pear and adding 1 teaspoon ground ginger. Top with a slice of pear.

elderflower ice milk
Prepare the basic recipe but replace the passion fruit with 1 cup elderflower cordial and omit the honey. Top with a slice of fruit or a sprig of elderflower.

ricotta ice with roasted figs

see base recipe page 264

ricotta ice with roasted pears
Prepare the basic recipe, replacing the figs with 3 ripe pears, peeled, cored, and quartered before roasting. Save 4 pieces of pear for serving.

ricotta ice with roasted quince
Replace the figs of the basic recipe with 3 ripe quinces, peeled, cored, and quartered. Add the juice of 1 orange when roasting the quinces, and roast them until tender, about 20 minutes. Save 4 pieces of quinces for serving.

ricotta ice with prunes
Prepare the basic recipe, replacing the figs with about 24 pitted, dried prunes. Serve the ice with 1 or 2 roasted prunes per serving.

ricotta ice with roasted apricots
Prepare the basic recipe, replacing the figs with 12 large ripe pitted apricots.

variations

frosty summer pudding

see base recipe page 267

frosty red summer pudding
Prepare the basic recipe, using only red fruits—strawberries, cranberries, and red currants—and adding extra sugar or sweetener if you wish.

frosty currant summer pudding
Prepare the basic recipe, this time using only currants—black, red, white—and adding extra sugar to taste.

frosty orchard fruit summer pudding
Prepare the basic recipe, replacing the summer fruits with peeled, sliced, and frozen apples, pears, and plums. Replace the allspice with ground cinnamon.

frosty blackberry & apple summer pudding
Prepare the basic recipe, replacing the summer fruits with equal quantities of apples (peeled, cored, sliced, and frozen) and frozen blackberries. Replace the allspice with ground cinnamon.

frosty apricot & peach summer pudding
When preparing the basic recipe, replace the summer fruits with peeled, sliced, and frozen ripe apricots, nectarines, and peaches. Replace the allspice with ground nutmeg.

frozen banana mango smoothie

see base recipe page 268

frozen bananaberry smoothie
Prepare the basic recipe, replacing the mango flesh with 2 cups of berries or mixed berries.

frozen banana plum smoothie
Replace the mango flesh of the basic recipe with 2 cups pitted plums.

frozen banana apple smoothie
Prepare the basic recipe, replacing the mango flesh with the pulp of 2 baked apples.

frozen banana pineapple smoothie
When preparing the basic recipe, replace the mango flesh with 2 cups chopped pineapple.

frozen banana cherry smoothie
Prepare the basic recipe, but replace the mango flesh with 2 cups pitted sweet red cherries.

variations

iced margarita

see base recipe page 271

iced cranberry margarita
Prepare the basic recipe, replacing the lime juice with cranberry juice.

iced blood orange margarita
When preparing the basic recipe, replace the lime juice with blood orange juice.

iced raspberry margarita
Prepare the basic recipe, replacing the lime juice with strained raspberry purée. If you wish, replace the salt with superfine sugar.

iced golden margarita
Prepare the basic recipe, adding 1/4 cup mango or papaya juice to the tequila and lime juice before freezing. If you wish, replace the salt with superfine sugar.

iced coconut margarita
Prepare the basic recipe and add 1/4 cup coconut milk to the tequila and lime juice before freezing.

variations

buck's fizz granita

see base recipe page 272

bellini granita
Prepare the basic recipe, replacing the orange juice with peach juice. Serve
with a slice of fresh peach.

kiwi fizz granita
Prepare the basic recipe but replace the orange juice with kiwi juice.

summer fizz granita
Replace the orange juice of basic recipe with the strained juice of
summer berries.

strawberry kir granita
Prepare the basic recipe, replacing the orange juice with strained strawberry
juice and adding a shot or small measure of cassis before freezing.

melon fizz granita
When preparing the basic recipe, replace the orange juice with puréed and
sieved melon and add a shot or small measure of Midori or melon liqueur
before freezing.

index